GERMAN VISITORS TO ENGLISH THEATERS
IN THE EIGHTEENTH CENTURY

GERMAN VISITORS
TO ENGLISH THEATERS
IN THE EIGHTEENTH CENTURY

By
JOHN ALEXANDER KELLY

PRINCETON UNIVERSITY PRESS · PRINCETON · 1936
HUMPHREY MILFORD · OXFORD UNIVERSITY PRESS · LONDON

ACKNOWLEDGMENTS

M ANY of the sources of this study are rare. Consequently I have required a great deal of assistance in finding them. It is a pleasure to acknowledge my indebtedness to a number of librarians in the Staatsbibliothek and the Universitätsbibliothek in Berlin, the Nationalbibliothek and the Universitätsbibliothek in Vienna, the Staatsbibliothek in Munich, and the British Museum.

In the preparation of the manuscript I have had the generous and wise counsel of Professor Robert Herndon Fife, of Columbia University, and Professor George Madison Priest, of Princeton University. To both I am truly grateful for this assistance, and to Professor Priest also for his patient and efficient reading of the proof.

JOHN ALEXANDER KELLY,
HAVERFORD, PENNSYLVANIA

CONTENTS

INTRODUCTION

IF any one document may be said to mark a turning-point in the history of a whole literature, certainly it is the seventeenth *Literaturbrief* of Lessing. Here the young critic breaks once for all with the pseudo-classic tradition of France, which had long dominated German letters, and directs his fellow countrymen to English models for guidance, declaring that the German spirit is much more closely akin to the English than to the French. Once accepted, English influence, with Shakespeare contributing the main current, was to change the whole course of German literature. This literary revolution, reaching its blatant climax in the *Sturm und Drang,* affects works of every type, but most of all the drama, a genre ardently cultivated by the young "geniuses" of the period. To Lenz, the typical *Stürmer und Dränger,* as to Goethe in his youth, Shakespeare is everything. Lenz especially would throw rules and restrictions of every description to the winds, even the hitherto sacred dramatic unities along with the rest. In his *Anmerkungen übers Theater* he demands for the new literature the "imitation of nature," which he defines simply as the "imitation of Shakespeare." The representative plays of the day are vaguely styled "English pieces," and Lenz and Klinger and their confrères easily out-English the English in looseness of composition and in their efforts towards the exact reproduction of "nature."

In view of this boundless enthusiasm for English drama, it seems worth while to review the first-hand impressions of Germans who visited English theaters in those days. The published accounts of their travels were widely read at home, for the German interest in foreign culture, certainly a national characteristic, was then already fully aroused. Second only to the Englishman, the German was the globe-trotter of the eighteenth century, and from that day to this the Ger-

mans more than any other people have sought to understand
and assimilate the intellectual life of foreign countries. It is
true, perhaps, that they have sometimes overestimated the
success of their efforts along these lines. They have frequently
set themselves up as the authoritative interpreters of the cultural achievements of the different nations, holding that Germany is a sort of intellectual melting-pot for the civilized
world. But no one can question the industry, enthusiasm and
intelligence they have brought to this ambitious task.

The following comments on dramatic works, actors and
playhouses, many of them gleaned from the writings of otherwise unknown travellers, present not a great deal that is new
and valuable as a contribution to the history of the English
stage. Here and there, to be sure, may be found entertaining
and sometimes enlightening discussions of the staging and
performance of certain plays, the merits of actors in certain
rôles, the audiences, and, less frequently, the pieces themselves. Since many of the tourists were familiar with the
leading theaters on the Continent, especially those of Paris,
they sometimes make illuminating comparisons of the London stage with others, thus presenting at least a slight positive
contribution to English theatrical history. Most of what they
say, however, may be found more fully and reliably recorded
in some of the numerous English memoirs of the times, or
in contemporary criticisms in newspapers and other periodicals.[1] On the other hand, the very fact that as foreigners they
witness the performances from a different and often original
point of view lends interest to their comments. Furthermore
the effect of these reports upon their German readers cannot
have been negligible. They are certainly important as a source
of English influence upon the German drama, as many small
tributaries to that great stream of which the main course has
already been thoroughly charted by a host of scholars.

Perhaps the present study will be of interest chiefly as a
cultural picture, in that it reveals the German mind in the

[1] See Gray, C. H., *Theatrical Criticism in London to 1795*, New York,
Columbia University Press, 1931.

eighteenth century by means of its reaction to a great foreign institution. When we remind ourselves that the first of our travellers came from a Germany which was only beginning to recover materially and spiritually from the ravages of the Thirty Years' War, and that the last of them came from that great Germany which for at least a brief period under the leadership of Goethe and Schiller could justly lay claim to supremacy in modern literature, we may expect to be able to observe a remarkable mental evolution. Generally speaking, such an evolution is plainly discernible. To be sure, we shall encounter a few men of some enlightenment in the early decades of the century, and shall still find men of limited vision towards its close, but as a whole our investigation reflects the gradual advancement of culture in Germany throughout the period we shall cover. Despite the great contribution of the two towering figures, Voltaire and Rousseau, and other Frenchmen to this development, it is safe to say that England was the chief educator of the German mind in the eighteenth century. Hence the importance of the German reaction to English culture can scarcely be exaggerated.

Among the travellers whose comments are to be presented are playwrights of some importance, dramatic critics recognized in Germany, and at least one theatrical producer. These men undoubtedly conveyed to Germany in one way or another something of the English stage tradition, hence their connection with the theater will be noted. In addition some account of the tourists themselves will be given, and of their general impressions of the English scene, in the belief that such apparent digressions will be of interest in themselves and will also have some bearing on the specific discussions of the theaters. Whenever feasible the sources will be quoted verbatim, usually through the medium of the English language.

I have sought to avoid useless duplication of material already accessible in various works on German visitors to

England.[2] A certain amount of repetition seemed desirable, however, in order to give coherence to my narrative. At the same time I have treated somewhat more fully than strict adherence to my subject warrants, perhaps, certain travellers who have not been included in previous studies. I have taken this liberty because it seemed worth while to call attention to some of the views of these forgotten men. Furthermore, I have accepted as Germans all natives of the German language region who have come up for my consideration except Friedrich Melchior Grimm, the *encyclopédiste*. I omitted him, although he visited England towards the end of Garrick's career and reported to Diderot on the English theater, because he definitely cast his lot with France. I have included such men as Muralt and Meister, although they are more closely identified with French than German culture, because they were German trained and their works were published originally and widely circulated in German territory. In addition to them Pöllnitz, Bielfeld, Hartig, Reinhold Forster and Wimpffen wrote of their travel impressions in French, calling attention again to the persistence of that language as a cultural tongue in Germany. They are, however, definitely German, although Wimpffen is less so than the others. At least in Forster's case the French style is bad enough to remove any doubts. My chief sources of information as to the men themselves are *Die allgemeine deutsche Biographie* and Meusel's *Das gelehrte Teutschland*. Other sources, and occasionally these two as well, are mentioned in the footnotes.

[2] The following works treat from various angles the impressions of German visitors to England in the eighteenth century:

Elsasser, Robert, *Ueber die politischen Bildungsreisen der Deutschen nach England,* Heidelberg, 1917.

Kelly, J. A., *England and the Englishman in German Literature of the Eighteenth Century,* New York, Columbia University Press, 1921.

Matheson, P. A., *German Visitors to England 1770-1795,* Taylorian Lecture, 1930. Oxford, Clarendon Press, 1930.

Muncker, Franz, *Anschauungen vom englischen Staat und Volk in der deutschen Literatur der letzten vier Jahrhunderte,* I. Teil, Von Erasmus bis zu Goethe und den Romantikern, München, 1918.

Phillipsthal, Robert, *Deutsche Reisende des XVIII. Jahrhunderts in England,* in Festschrift zum 13. Allgemeinen Deutschen Neuphilologentage, Hannover, 1908.

CHAPTER I

EARLY VISITORS

A GLANCE into a few German *Reisebeschreibungen* of the late seventeenth century readily convinces us that little is to be learned from them regarding the theaters or for that matter any other aspect of English culture. These works, as well as many belonging to the same category in the eighteenth century, especially the first half of it, are for the most part models of superficiality and shallowness. If we compare them with those of a later date, we find in general a marked improvement both as to content and style. It is, in fact, in just such literary byways as we are to explore that the gradual dawn of the Age of Enlightenment is most apparent. Typical of the obscure gentlemen of the darker age is Adam Paul Ebert, who was a professor of law in his native city of Frankfurt-an-der-Oder and is, or was, known chiefly for his long, crack-brained will, in which he bequeathed his *Geist* to all scholars in the whole of Europe. In his old age he published under the pseudonym Aulus Apronius an account of the extensive travels of his youth.[1] A modest inscription adorns the title-page: "Zur Freude der Welt und ewiger Zeiten." Ebert was in London from Easter to October 1674. He saw at "Morfiels [*sic*] the insane secretary of the famous Milton," and observed that doors in London were constructed with ten keyholes for the purpose of confusing burglars, that the Quakers practised communism of property and wives, and that Westminster Abbey was "a large old building." He advises everyone except theologians and merchants against visiting England, on the ground that nothing is to be seen in that country save London, and London is as nothing in comparison with Paris. He informs us that one of the theaters

[1] *Reisebeschreibung von Villa Franca der Chur-Brandenburg durch Teutschland, Holland und Brabant, England . . . etc.* Frankfurt-an-der-Oder, 1723. pp. 45-93 are devoted to England.

is situated on the Thames. Eagerly we look for his impressions of the Restoration stage, but instead we are treated with a description of the river and learn that Sunday is a very dull day in London.

The *Reisebeschreibung* of Johann Limberg[2] is unique in that the author intertwines with itineraries and dry descriptions of countries and cities, museums and curiosities, an account of his own life over a period of eighteen years. From 1667 to 1675 Limberg studied in turn at Marburg, Erfurt and Halle, beginning then his career as soldier, teacher and clergyman, Catholic and Protestant in turn. He travelled extensively, visiting England in 1677.[3] For that country and its inhabitants he has only praise. Unlike Ebert he considers London the most beautiful city in the world. Of the theater he has not a word to say. In fact, there is no good reason why he should not have produced his description of England in the seclusion of his German study without ever taking the trouble to cross the Channel. Thus, as in the case of Wagner's *Rheingold,* our view of English theaters through German eyes begins with a thoughtful pause at zero grade.

The first important figure we meet is Beat Ludwig Muralt (1665-1749). He was a native of Bern, where he resided until his deistic views, acquired in part in England, led to his banishment. After a brief period in Geneva, where he again got into difficulties on account of his religious leanings, he finally settled in the little village Colombier in Neuchâtel. While travelling in France and England in 1694-1695, he recorded his impressions and experiences in letters to a friend. Years later, as he was entering upon his exile, he destroyed these letters, but it happened that copies of some or all of them were preserved, and the author finally was prevailed upon to publish them. Some of them appeared in 1712 in French,

---

[2] *Denkwürdige Reisebeschreibung durch Teutschland, Italien, Portugal, Engelland, Frankreich und Schweitz,* Leipzig, 1690. pp. 647-74 treat of England.

[3] See *Fortsetzung und Ergänzungen zu Christian Gottlieb Jöchers allgemeinem Gelehrten-Lexikon,* Delmenhorst, 1810, Bd. 3, p. 1831.

the complete collection in 1725.[4] The work went through many editions and was soon translated into German and English. It is by far the most important of such works before that of Voltaire. Its influence in Germany was enormous.[5] Muralt's description of England is fairly objective. He frequently expresses his admiration for English common sense. He seems on the one hand to have been most favorably impressed by the pleasant life of the country gentleman with his material and intellectual independence, and on the other hand most profoundly shocked by the immorality of the metropolis. He gives to Continental readers the first intelligent discussion of the London stage,[6] consequently his criticism is reproduced here in some detail. Like most foreigners he was struck by the popularity of theatrical performances, which he found to be the chief form of amusement not only for the upper classes but for the common people as well. Despite the English claim of surpassing even the Ancients in comedy, Muralt is of the opinion that everyone who has taste and a preference for what is natural, in short, everyone "who is accustomed to Molière," will find little to please him in English comedies. The best of them, he says, are those of Ben Jonson, who, to be sure, was a great poet, yet inferior in many respects to Molière. Ben Jonson's unpardonable sin is that he made no attempt to correct the national faults. "He did much to improve English comedy, but nothing to improve the English." Comedy should correct follies by making them appear ridiculous, a fact well known in that day of Boileau's rule. If the English playwright fulfilled this obligation at all, he almost invariably sought his victims abroad, showing up the foibles of the Frenchman or at best of the Englishman who had assumed French manners. If perchance he ventured

[4] *Lettres sur les Anglois et les François, et sur les Voiages,* 3 vols., 1725. The revised edition of 1726 is cited here.

[5] See Muncker, F., *Anschauungen vom englischen Staat und Volk in der deutschen Literatur der letzten vier Jahrhunderte,* Part I, pp. 39-41. This admirable study discusses all tourists to England who hold an important position in the history of German literature.

[6] *Lettres,* Vol. I, pp. 40*ff.*

to attack native vices, he chose such unnatural and exaggerated examples that no spectator ever recognized them as his own. Hence English comedy was "useless." In fact, worse still: a source of the corruption of London. On this last point modern readers of Restoration drama will scarcely gainsay the Swiss critic. He considers the practice of author's benefit performances in part accountable for the low moral tone of the stage. To swell the box receipts the playwright descends to the coarsest humor, by means of which he hopes to induce even lackeys to pay the price of admission.

Anticipating the naturalistic trend of Diderot and even of Zola and his age, Muralt holds that nature should be so carefully reproduced on the stage as to conceal art altogether. Here again English comedy falls short, for the poet persists in making himself heard through the characters of his creation:[7]

> If you have ever seen a marionette play, imagine an unskilled performer who is unable for any length of time to adjust his voice to the stature of the little figures, but lets it escape from time to time and is heard to speak in his natural tone. The artifice is thus revealed, and the spell is broken. This is the English poet. He disillusions the spectator again and again, reminding him forcibly that he is at the theater.

The English, he continues, pride themselves above all things on their wealth of imagination, claiming that a French poet would spin out into an entire play thoughts which they would scarcely find sufficient for a single act. He recognizes that the English are unsurpassed in "sustained conversations and happy and forceful thoughts," but for his part he prefers the stricter economy of the French. What he cannot forgive is the maltreatment to which Molière is subjected in England. Shadwell's adaptation of *L'Avare,* for instance, is totally lacking in the subtlety and grace of the original. Nor does Muralt take much stock in the *humour* which the English claim as their peculiar merit. He defines the word as approxi-

[7] *Lettres,* Vol. I, p. 49.

mately the same thing as the *bons mots* of the French, and
"precisely what we call *Einfall*." But whatever the literal
meaning of the word, it seems to him that "they mean by it
a certain fertility of imagination which usually tends to dis-
tort the idea of things, making virtue appear ridiculous and
vice attractive." And again we hear the *leitmotif* of his criticism of English comedy. He reiterates that he looks upon the
theater as a means of correcting faults and that he suffers
when he sees comedy only confirming them. "If England had
had her Molière instead of all these poets with their *humours,*
perhaps the people would have corrected some great fault,
for example, their readiness to show their contempt for the
rest of the world."[8]

English tragedy appeals a bit more to Muralt than English
comedy. Since his views anticipate in part Voltaire's and prevailed widely in Germany until they gave way to Lessing's
criticism, they are given at length:[9]

> If the English could make up their minds to be simple
> and to study more carefully the language of nature, they
> would doubtless surpass all the nations of Europe in
> tragedy. England is a country of passions and catas-
> trophes, so much so that *Schakspear,* one of their best
> ancient poets, has put a large part of their history into
> tragedies. Furthermore, the genius of the nation is seri-
> ous, and the language is succinct and vigorous and well
> adapted to the expression of passion. Their tragedies
> abound accordingly in excellent passages. But they have
> the same faults as their comedies and, I think, others be-
> sides. In them the heroes of antiquity are travestied as in
> France. Hannibal appears in a long powdered wig, with
> his helmet on, with ribbons on his tabard, and holding
> his sword in a fringed glove. The plays, as well as the
> characters, are a mixture of comic and serious elements.
> The saddest events and the most absurd farces succeed
> one another. . . . Finally, the majority of the execu-
> tions which are represented in their tragedies take place
> on the stage, which is often strewn with dead bodies.

[8] *Lettres,* Vol. I, p. 64.
[9] *ibid.,* p. 66.

Against all these practices Muralt protests in strong language. Still less does he condone the persistent attacks of the English on French authors, "whose sole offense is to surpass them." Their most famous contemporary tragic poet treats Corneille no better than *Schadvel* treats Molière, that is, pillages him and writes prefaces to speak ill of him.[10]

As for opera in London, Muralt considered the music mediocre, the stage machinery neither better nor worse than in Paris, and the scenery excellent, at times magnificent. The ballets were not so good as in France, but, by way of compensation, were less frequent and better timed. Only the arias were sung, the rest was recited. The arias were usually "pleasing but sad." The concerts were on a higher plane musically than the operas, an observation made by many tourists. Although Muralt found much to admire in England, he unexpectedly concludes his last letter by advising his friend not to do that usual and useless thing, namely to take a trip to England.

The first German tourist to give an account of actual performances which he witnessed in London was Zacharias Conrad von Uffenbach (1683-1737). He belonged to a patrician family of Frankfurt to which Goethe pays tribute in *Dichtung und Wahrheit*.[11] He studied at Strassburg and Halle in preparation for the legal profession and became a councillor of his native city. In this position he was for the last ten years of his life a colleague of Goethe's grandfather, Johann Wolfgang Textor. Uffenbach acquired one of the largest and most valuable private collections of books and manuscripts of his day and was noted for his generosity in placing it at the disposal of the public. In so doing he was emulating an English custom which had won his admiration.[12] Uffenbach set out

[10] Muralt refers presumably to Dryden, who in collaboration with Lee wrote an *Oedipus,* based on Sophocles and Seneca as well as Corneille. In the preface Dryden writes disparagingly of Corneille's *Oedipe.*

[11] Weimar ed., 1, Vol. XXVI, p. 114.

[12] *Merkwürdige Reisen durch Niedersachsen, Holland und Engelland,* 3 vols., Vol. I, Frankfurt und Leipzig, 1753; Vols. II-III, Ulm, 1753-1754. See Vol. II, p. 565.

with his younger brother in November 1709 on the trip which took him to England for the purpose of "increasing his knowledge and enlarging his book collection." He was in England from June 5 to November 5, 1710, and spent the months of August and September at Oxford and Cambridge. He writes at length on the universities and on the scholars whom he met.

The first play which Uffenbach attended was Thomas Baker's *Yeoman of Kent*[13] at the Haymarket on June 11. On the strength of this first impression he declares that English comedies are unsurpassed and that the acting is remarkably good and natural. The play pleased him, but he saw others more to his liking later. Having learned French mainly by attending the Strassburg theaters, he was resolved to learn English by the same method and made it a rule to read the texts in advance and to carry them with him to the performances. On June 13 Uffenbach saw at Drury Lane Shadwell's *The fair Quaker of Deal,* for which he has high praise. It seemed to him very curious, "since the English Quakers and Quakeresses are represented quite realistically in it."[14] He commends Miss Santlow for her beauty and still more for her skill in acting and especially in dancing, but he is not so well pleased with what he has heard as to her character. Both of this performance and others he describes the varied entertainments interpolated in the plays. He is astonished on one occasion by the enthusiastic reception of a song in which the Duke of Marlborough is derided as a miser, and at that, in the Queen's Theatre and in the presence of the distinguished but then unpopular general's wife, the Duchess of Marl-

[13] The title turns up in Uffenbach's diary as *You Man of Kent.* Baker's *Tunbridge-Walks; or, The Yeoman of Kent,* first performed at Drury Lane, January 1702/3, was revived at the Haymarket May 29, 1710.

[14] German visitors to England were interested in the Quakers even before Voltaire published his letters on them. Uffenbach took an early opportunity to attend Quaker meeting and seemed disappointed to find "no great difference between the Quakers here and those in Amsterdam." *Tagebuch,* Vol. II, p. 552.

borough.[15] Of Ravenscroft's *The London Cuckolds*, which he saw on June 16, he simply states that it is "a merry and pleasing piece and always draws a large crowd." On June 20 he saw Ben Jonson's *The silent Woman*,[16] "in which a misanthrope is admirably portrayed." On July 20 he saw a comedy, *The Changes*,[17] but it elicited no comment. On July 17 it was "*The old Batchelor*, by Mr. Congreve, a merry comedy," and on July 24 Farquhar's *The recruiting Officer*, "one of the best and merriest pieces."

Apparently the Uffenbach brothers saw but one tragedy. On July 3: "Abends waren wir at the Queens Theatre in the Haymarket, und sahen *Othello Moor of Venice* written by the immortal Shakespear. Es war ein schönes Stück, auch desswegen voller Menschen."[18] The first review of a Shakespeare performance by a German witness is regrettably laconic. It appears, however, to have inspired him to try his hand, though cautiously, at the English language, as we have seen.

Of the one opera he attended Uffenbach has more to say. It was a performance of *Hidaspis*[19] at the Haymarket on the tenth of June, the last day of the season. He was impressed by the building itself and considered the opera remarkably beautiful in every respect, "in composition, music and presentation." He was convinced that even in Italy opera could not be better. The director, Nicolai, who had made a name for himself in Venice, was great. The orchestra was unsur-

---

[15] *Tagebuch*, Vol. I, p. 598. Uffenbach refers to the duchess as the general's daughter; but the Duchess of Marlborough, the famous Sarah Jennings, survived her husband by many years, until 1744.

[16] Source of Stefan Zweig's libretto to Richard Strauss' opera.

[17] A play entitled *The Changes, or Love in a Maze*, by James Shirley, was produced at the Theatre Royal on May 1, 1667. Uffenbach may have seen Beaumont and Fletcher's *The Chances*, probably with the alterations made in it by the Duke of Buckingham, which was given repeatedly at the Haymarket in 1710. Genest does not record any performances of *The Changes* in that year. See *English Stage*, Vol. I, p. 67; Vol. II, p. 455; Vol. IX, p. 546.

[18] By this last phrase Uffenbach doubtless means that the play was well attended.

[19] Francesco Mancini's *L'Idaspe fedele* was given a number of times at the Haymarket in 1710.

passable, but composed altogether of foreigners, "mainly Germans, and then Frenchmen; for the English are not much better musicians than the Dutch, that is to say, rather poor." All the singers were admirable in the execution of their rôles, especially Nicolini, "who in this respect surpasses all the actors in the world." The orchestra was directed by Pepusch, a Brandenburger, whom on another occasion Uffenbach heard in an excellent concert.[20]

The books of one Johann Basil Küchelbecker on foreign countries were apparently successful, for he persisted in publishing them.[21] Honest Saxon that he was, he surely did not write these volumes without visiting the countries of which they treat; yet he could conceivably have written them as well had he remained at his home in Oberlausitz, for most of his observations were already on record in various books of travel. A sort of forerunner of Baedeker, he gives benevolent rules for tourists. He would have them take their wanderings seriously, and not, as he puts it, just gaze at foreign countries as the cow at the new door. He includes theatrical performances among the dissipations of travellers,[22] but assures the lover of spectacles that he may have his fill of them in London, for besides the operas there are plays to be seen every day both at Drury Lane and the Haymarket. For his part he does not care for the English stage, and he believes that everyone will be of like mind who has seen "the Parisian plays and among them especially the incomparable tragedies, in which the French easily surpass all other nations." On the other hand Parisian opera is a *Kinderspiel* in comparison with English, both in composition and music,[23] and the singers in London, many of whom are Italians, are the best in the world. Only

[20] *Tagebuch*, Vol. II, p. 478.
[21] Information on Küchelbecker is scant. In Jöchers' *Fortsetzung*, Vol. III, p. 926, where he is called Kuchelbecker, it appears that he was *juris utriusque doctor* and the author of a legal treatise.
[22] *Der nach Engelland reisende curieuse Passagier, oder kurtze Beschreibung der Stadt London*, andere Auflage, vermehrt und verbessert, Hannover, 1736, p. 13.
[23] *ibid.*, p. 145.

in their ballets do the French excel. Admission to the London operas is expensive, to be sure, but the foreigner is justified in the outlay, "especially since their equal is not to be found in Germany, although the Hamburg opera is passable." In 1737 Küchelbecker published a second volume on England.[24] In it[25] he lists the great English writers as Sir Philip Sidney, Spenser, Samuel Daniel, Michael Drayton, Beaumont, Fletcher, and Ben Jonson, omitting, as was usually the case in his day, the name of Shakespeare. It does not appear just when Küchelbecker was in England. He speaks of the Haymarket Theatre as having been built "not a great while ago." It was built in 1704. He mentions Händel as the director of the opera. Händel resided in London most of his life after 1712. Alberti, from whom we shall hear later on, speaks of Küchelbecker's *Beschreibung von England* of the year 1717. It is not likely, however, that uncertainty as to this date will cause any grave concern.

Albrecht von Haller (1708-1777) was the first of the German visitors to England in the eighteenth century who may be said to occupy a permanently important position in the history of German letters. This famous Swiss scholar and littérateur who anticipated some of Rousseau's most important ideas and who was to achieve distinction as a scientist and to exert a wide influence as a professor at Göttingen, spent a few weeks in England in the summer of 1727, dividing his time between London and Oxford. The purpose of his trip was to make the acquaintance of foreign scholars and to advance his scientific studies. It was not until later that he acquired a thorough knowledge of the English language and literature. In the diary which he kept on his journey he seems to draw as much from Muralt as from personal observation, yet his impressions of land and people are consistently more favorable than those of his compatriot, and his admiration for the English political system knows no bounds. It is pre-

---

[24] *Allerneueste Nachricht vom Königreich Engelland,* Frankfurt und Leipzig, 1737.
[25] *ibid.,* p. 26.

cisely in literature, however, that the youthful Haller failed to see any greatness in England. The harshness of their language and the exclusive use of masculine rhymes seemed to him to disqualify the English for most types of literature. He holds that they have done but little in tragedy, "unless [Addison's] *Cato* and a few other pieces deserve fame, although the free and rather fierce spirit of the people is always in evidence."[26]

Of all the Germans who visited England in the first half of the century the poet Friedrich von Hagedorn was certainly the best qualified to write on the life and culture of the country, yet he is the very one of whose experiences and impressions no record has been preserved aside from a few general comments sprinkled here and there mainly in his poems. These fragmentary observations and opinions, however, are sufficient to show his strong English sympathies.

If we regret Haller's youthful superficiality and Hagedorn's silence, we shall have no occasion to complain of brevity in the case of Karl Ludwig Baron von Pöllnitz (1692-1775). He is prolix enough, but apparently his contemporaries were not always eager to hear what he had to say. Frederick the Great wrote to Voltaire on the occasion of Pöllnitz' death that he was lamented by nobody save his creditors.[27] He seems to have been one of those eccentric adventurers produced so lavishly by the eighteenth century, a spiritual kinsman of Casanova and Beaumarchais, but unfortunately without their genius. A descendant of a natural daughter of William I of Orange, he tried his luck at gambling and in various amours, borrowing money wherever he could and repaying it never. He was at one time chamberlain at the court of Frederick William I of Prussia, and after the accession of Frederick II in 1740 was for a while Master of Ceremonies. But he was never able to cast anchor anywhere

---

[26] Haller's diary was not published until 1883; *Tagebücher seiner Reise nach Deutschland, Holland und England, 1723-1727,* hrsg. von L. Hirzel, Leipzig, 1883. See p. 113.

[27] *Oeuvres complètes de Voltaire,* Paris, 1832, Vol. LII, p. 313.

for very long. He is the first of our *Englandfahrer* to write with a view to publication and the first to appear promptly in print. Ebert's trivial observations were withheld from the public for nearly a half century, Muralt's letters appeared thirty years after they were written, Uffenbach's diary forty-five years after his visit to England; and Haller's diary remained in manuscript for a century and a half. In the case of some similar writings later on, publication was likewise long deferred; so that whatever effect they might have had on the German mind was accordingly diminished. We shall see, however, that the travellers offer the accounts of their journeys more promptly to the public as the interest in things English increases, and the steadily swelling volume of "literature" on the subject is itself a fairly accurate gauge of the rise of anglomania in Germany.

Pöllnitz' *Mémoires,* written in French, appeared in 1734[28] and went through five editions in the five years following. The first German edition appeared in 1735 and the most recent in 1900. Another of his books, *La Saxe galante,* also saw many editions and reprints, including one of recent date. Much of Pöllnitz' early life is shrouded in obscurity. This is particularly true of his *Wanderjahre,* which covered the period 1710-1723. His English memoirs purport to have been written on the basis of observations made chiefly in the year 1733, but the date is not to be taken too seriously. In our day of propaganda and enlightenment the author might appear to be in the pay of the British government. He frequently compares England with France and Italy, and England usually comes out triumphant. He enjoys London more than Paris, yet admits with apparent reluctance that Paris is the most beautiful city in Europe.[29] For a man reared in the French literary tradition as he had been, Pöllnitz is surprisingly open-minded as regards London theaters. He cites the fact that the English have more spectacles than any other nation as evidence of their fondness for them. Their Italian

28 Three vols., Liège, 1734.
29 *Mémoires,* Vol. III, p. 403.

opera he considers "the best and most magnificent in Europe."[30] He has in fact no fault to find with it except the small matter of the music, "which is ordinarily composed by one Händel" and is too intellectual to suit the Prussian courtier's taste. Henceforth Germans in London will frequently mention Händel's music, but only in terms of praise. Pöllnitz enjoyed English opera, of which only the arias were sung, the rest being recited. Of this he particularly approves, "for a man does not sing while in the act of killing himself or of fighting." If he was in London in 1733, he undoubtedly saw *The Beggar's Opera,* for it was performed repeatedly in that year.[31]

Pöllnitz' remarks on English tragedy[32] are of especial interest, since they antedate slightly the appearance of Voltaire's *Lettres philosophiques,* which moulded Continental opinion on English literature for a full generation:

English comedy is highly esteemed by the English and has been severely criticized by the French, who consider it by no means comparable with their own. The *beaux esprits* of the two countries have treated this important subject very seriously and have appeared equally presumptuous. I do not propose to decide between them. However, I do not hesitate to say that the French are in my opinion too much hampered by their rules and that the English are not sufficiently restrained. Thus the two nations show their difference in taste, the one for submission, the other for liberty. It seems to me that the English abound in happy thoughts, even if they do not adhere to unity of action and unity of place. Besides, however prejudiced they may be in favor of their own productions, they are not lacking in appreciation of those French plays in which they find ideas that are acceptable to them. They have just translated the tragedy *Brutus,* by Voltaire. This play has been even more successful in London than in Paris.

[30] *Mémoires,* Vol. II, pp. 302ff., on opera in Italy.
[31] See Nicoll, A., *A History of Early 18th Century Drama, 1700-1750,* Cambridge University Press, 1929, p. 331.
[32] *Mémoires,* Vol. III, pp. 420f.

Pöllnitz adds that Voltaire, under the influence of English liberty, had forgotten that he was a Frenchman while writing his *Brutus,* hence "kings speak as if they were men." It is a well known fact that Voltaire approaches the "Shakespeare style" in this drama as closely as his own taste and the indulgence of his Continental public will allow. Pöllnitz' remarks on a performance of the play which he witnessed at St. Cyr are of interest.[33] He attended the theater in company with some English friends, and they were all delighted not only with the construction and style of the play, but also with the freedom of thought and speech which the author allows his Romans. But the French did not approve:

> The respect due to royalty is not observed, they say. They cannot forgive the author his daring to confine royal authority within the limits of justice. It is not in France that M. de Voltaire has imbibed these sentiments. It is easy enough to see that they were imported from across the sea. They might do very well for the English, but to us they are quite intolerable, and if M. de Voltaire continues to write in this vein, he may eventually occupy an apartment in the Bastille.

In his comparison of French and English tragedy Pöllnitz states the problem of which Lessing is to give the classical solution some thirty-five years later. Yet while the author of the *Hamburgische Dramaturgie* takes sides positively with the English, the fact remains that he cautiously follows in his own dramatic masterpieces the middle course of which Pöllnitz approved, avoiding on the one hand the rigid rules of French drama and on the other the freedom of English. The ultimate result of Lessing's criticism, and doubtless the conscious purpose of it, was to emancipate German drama from all foreign influence. Hitherto the only question that could be expected to arise was whether French classicism was authentic in its embodiment of the principles of Aristotle and the Greek tragedians. Gottsched had for his generation settled any possible doubts on that score. But Lessing sets

---

[33] Letter, Paris, May 12, 1732.

up Shakespeare as a standard of perfection beside and opposed
to the classical tradition. Confronted thus by conflicting
authorities, the German dramatist must eventually learn to
go his own way, with his own genius as his most reliable
guide. That the "genius" of the *Stürmer und Dränger* ran
away with them was not Lessing's fault.

Baron Jacob Friedrich von Bielfeld (1717-1770), who
spent the first half of the year 1741 in London as a member
of the Prussian Embassy, expresses as great admiration for
England as Pöllnitz does, and at the very time when Frederick
the Great was zealously engaged in Frenchifying his court.
Bielfeld had previously visited England in the year 1737. His
letters on England are addressed to Hagedorn, Pöllnitz and
other Germans who were especially interested in English culture, and are dedicated to Voltaire with attestations of the
highest esteem and admiration.[34] Bielfeld adored Madame
Gottsched, praised Gellert's *Schwedische Gräfin,* knew and
personally esteemed Glover, whom he considered the only
great poet in England after Pope's death, and had admiration
left over for both Richardson and Fielding, difficult as it was
in those times to bracket the two together. His literary taste,
however, was essentially French, and his highest approval
was bestowed on Voltaire, Gottsched, "die Gottschedin" and
Madame Neuber.[35] Bielfeld was indeed an ever affirming
spirit. He wrote voluminously on a variety of subjects, his
most important work being *Frederick the Great and his
Court.*

Bielfeld likens the English to the ancient Romans in that
they require for their contentment only bread and spectacles.[36]
Besides tragedies and comedies, operas and concerts, they enjoyed horse races, bull fights, dog fights and even cock fights.

[34] *Lettres familières et autres,* La Haye, 1763; 2nd German ed., *Freund-
schaftliche Briefe,* Danzig und Leipzig, 1770. References are to the French
edition.
[35] See his *Progrès des Allemands dans les Sciences, les Belles-Lettres
et les Arts* (Berlin), 1752; pp. 188-243, "Du Théâtre allemand." German
trans. in *Theaterjournal für Deutschland,* 14. Stück, Gotha, 1780.
[36] *Lettres familières,* Vol. I, p. 273.

The baron did not care for these more vulgar amusements, but he had greater enthusiasm for the London stage than one would expect to find in Gottsched's school:[37]

> The first time I saw an English tragedy performed, the gestures of the actors seemed to me grotesque, and the sound of their voices roared frightfully in my ears. But although I still consider their declamation on the whole too extravagant, I am no longer shocked by it. I even discover truthfulness in it sometimes, and invariably an extraordinary power which in the more pathetic passages of the plays is most effective. I could wish, however, that the actors would vary their tone somewhat more, thereby approaching more closely to nature and avoiding a certain monotony in their declamation to which I shall never become accustomed. English comedy is my delight. I find in it an admirable liveliness and naturalness which other nations in their over-scrupulous subservience to rules of art are unable to achieve.

Bielfeld notes with pleasure the popularity of Voltaire's dramas in London.[38] He also comments on the theater directors and some of the actors, including Mlle. Barberina, subsequently a favorite at the court of Frederick the Great. She is described as "a Venus for beauty and a Terpsichore in the dance."[39] The musical piece *Comus,* by John Dalton, was quite to Bielfeld's liking. In fact, he declared that he had never enjoyed anything so much in his life and that he was resolved to learn all the airs by heart.[40] As for opera in general, he finds that it has declined decidedly since his visit to London five years earlier, when Händel and Heidegger were vying with one another in the production of Italian works, making London "the seat of music." But now it seems that

[37] *Lettres familières,* Vol. I, p. 267.
[38] *ibid.,* p. 290. Voltaire's plays were not conspicuously popular on the London stage. See Bruce, H. L., *Voltaire on the English Stage,* University of California Publications in Modern Philology, Vol. VIII, no. 1, 1918, pp. 140*ff.*
[39] *Lettres familières,* Vol. I, p. 268.
[40] *ibid.,* p. 269.

"Euterpe has abandoned the shores of Albion." One can find some compensation now and then in a Händel oratorio.

Georg Wilhelm Alberti (1723-1758) was apparently the first of the German visitors to England, excepting perhaps Hagedorn, whose command of the language was entirely adequate for his reporting on theatrical performances. After studying theology for more than three years at Göttingen, he went in 1745 to England to continue his studies, and remained there until 1747. He had prepared himself by a careful perusal of Muralt, Voltaire and other writers on England and had even gleaned what he could from Küchelbecker, the only contemporary German authority whom he cites. Encouraged by the favorable reception of his modest *Nachricht von den Quäkern,* which he published in 1750, he promptly undertook to treat of the whole field of English culture and for the purpose allowed himself 1367 printed pages.[41] He found much to admire in England, particularly religious liberty, enlightenment and scientific progress. He exerts himself to give a fair, unbiased account of everything,[42] but he views the stage in particular through the eyes of the Protestant clergyman and is so shocked by its immorality that he pays but little attention to any merits it may possess. He is convinced that "the difference between the former generation and the present" is only too apparent,[43] and he seizes upon the theater as the most conspicuous symptom of the deplorable degeneration. Holding that the spirit and morals of a people are most plainly reflected in their public amusements, he can form no high opinion of his English contemporaries, for their chief delight is precisely their immoral stage. They flock to the theaters in such numbers that one must arrive two hours in advance of the performance in order to secure a good seat.[44] It is evident that the young clergyman took many opportunities to convince himself of the degeneracy of the stage. He

[41] *Briefe betreffende* [sic] *den allerneuesten Zustand der Religion und der Wissenschaften in Grossbrittanien,* 4 vols., Hannover, 1752-1754.
[42] *ibid.,* Vol. II, p. 296.
[43] *ibid.,* Vol. II, p. 318.
[44] *ibid.,* Vol. II, p. 291.

lists as the most popular plays of the day Vanbrugh's *The provok'd Wife*, Benjamin Hoadly's *The suspicious Husband*, Garrick's *Miss in her Teens*, Rowe's *The fair Penitent*, Steele's *The conscious Lovers*, William Grimstone's *Love in a hollow Tree*,[45] Rowe's *Jane Shore*, and Addison's *Cato*. He examines several of these pieces from the moralist's point of view. Typical of his method is the following analysis :[46]

> The *Miss in her Teens* represents a maiden who in her sixteenth year is a finished coquette, and at that quite according to natural impulses; with this lovely moral, that however much care parents may give to the education of young girls, nature will frustrate all their efforts. . . . An actor named Garrick composed this play in 1746, and despite its ignoble drift, it met with extraordinary approval. The author himself calls it a "trifle," . . . which is the only true word in the play.

The repentance of the heroine in *Jane Shore,* the tears she sheds over her sins, and her prayers for forgiveness would strike a sympathetic chord in Alberti's heart, were the part not played by Mrs. Pritchard, "a public whore who is by no means inclined to abandon her dissolute life." On this account the whole performance seems to him blasphemous. With Addison's *Cato* he has no fault to find except that it confirms Englishmen in their sad proclivity to suicide.[47] The actors, this critic admits, have brought their art to a high degree of perfection and perform their rôles "right naturally." Outstanding among them are Garrick, Barry, Quin, Mrs. Pritchard, Mrs. Cibber and Mrs. Woffington. But their very proficiency only equips them the better for doing harm.[48] Alberti concurs with Muralt, whom he echoes, and with Bishop Burnet, whom he cites,[49] in the judgment that English plays with few exceptions tend to corrupt the morals of the people, particularly of the youth, and this in spite of the fact that the

[45] The full title is *The Lawyer's Fortune; or, Love in a hollow Tree.*
[46] *Briefe,* Vol. II, p. 292.
[47] *ibid.,* Vol. I, p. 80; Vol. II, p. 294.
[48] *ibid.,* Vol. II, p. 295.
[49] *ibid.,* Vol. II, p. 294.

history of the stage, which he outlines briefly, reveals it as a secular pulpit for the promulgation of "virtue, honesty and bravery." He claims that "wise Englishmen" agree with him in condemning the contemporary stage on moral grounds. And so they did.[50]

Alberti corroborates Bielfeld as to the decline of opera. There were still performances every Saturday at the Haymarket, he says, but they were not popular, as the texts were in Italian, all attempts to introduce opera in English having proved unsuccessful[51]—as they have on the whole down to the present day. He also touches on curious practices in London theaters, such as predetermining the reception of a new play, assuring at least the semblance of success by "packing the house with *claqueurs,* or of failure by arranging for a chorus of cat-calls and hisses." He warns foreigners not to take these first-night demonstrations too seriously.

Like Voltaire and many others who followed in his footsteps, Alberti is impressed by the homage paid to greatness in all fields. In the monument to Shakespeare in Westminster Abbey he sees a symbol of the British nation's appreciation of her distinguished sons and especially of her great poets.[52]

If Alberti saw the English stage through the eyes of the moralist, such was scarcely the case with Christlob Mylius (1722-1754). His reputation was not very good, and his moral standards were by no means too exacting. Lessing's parents considered him no fit associate for their son, and one Jonas Apelbald, a Swedish scholar, reported that Mylius had squandered his life and other people's money in London taverns.[53] In 1742 Mylius became a member of Gottsched's *Rednergesellschaft.* He took sides with the "Swan of Leip-

---

[50] See Gray, C. H., *op. cit.,* p. 103.
[51] cf. Nicoll, A., *op. cit.,* p. 236.
[52] *Briefe,* Vol. I, p. 93.
[53] See *Apelbalds Beschreibung seiner Reise durch Ober- und Niedersachsen und Hessen, 1755,* aus dem Schwedischen übersetzt von J. Bernoulli, Berlin und Leipzig, 1785, p. 317. There was quite a controversy as to Mylius' character. His friend, A. G. Kaestner, came to his defense in an article in *Physicalische Belustigungen,* 23. Stück, Berlin, 1754.

zig" in the famous controversy with Bodmer and Breitinger and contributed articles to the *Kritische Beiträge*. With Lessing, who was his cousin, he established the first German periodical devoted exclusively to the theater, the short-lived *Beiträge zur Historie und Aufnahme des Theaters*.[54] He also concocted several plays himself from the works of Molière and Holberg.[55] He played a rôle none too creditable in the Maupertuis-König affair, which was the occasion of the break between Voltaire and Frederick the Great. Voltaire wrote Gottsched[56] of a rumor to the effect that Mylius had been arrested in Holland *"sur une accusation d'affaires d'État."* Mylius' allegiance to Gottsched was of short duration, and he gradually turned from literature to the sciences. Under the patronage of the Berlin *Akademie der Wissenschaften* and with the especial support of Haller he set out on a trip to England and America for purposes of scientific research. He arrived in London on August 22, 1753, but got no farther, as he died there on March 7, 1754. Mylius did not spend all his time in the taverns. He went to church assiduously, heard Count von Zinsendorf deliver several sermons, and occasionally attended Quaker meeting. Under the author's supervision he prepared a translation of Hogarth's *Analysis of Beauty* which was published in 1754 under the title *Zergliederung der Schönheit*. He began his round of the places of amusement with Vauxhall, Marylebone, and again Vauxhall, and was well entertained at both places.[57]

At last we are to hear an account of a Shakespeare perform-

[54] See Hill, W., *Die deutschen Theaterschriften des 18. Jahrhunderts,* Forschungen zur neueren Literaturgeschichte, Weimar, 1915, p. 2.

[55] *Die Aerzte* (1745) ; *Der Unerträgliche* (1746) ; *Der Kuss* (1748), a musical *Schäferspiel* written at the request of Madame Neuber and frequently performed in Leipzig.

[56] April 19, 1753. Mylius claims (*Tagebuch,* April 28, 1753) to have received a letter from Voltaire telling him of the report that he, Mylius, had been hanged in Prussia for his complicity in the Maupertuis affair.

[57] *Tagebuch seiner Reise nach England,* in J. Bernoulli's Archiv zur neueren Geschichte, Geographie, Natur- und Menschenkunde, Vol. V, pp. 85-176; Vol. VI, pp. 39-140; Vol. VII, pp. 37-150; Vols. V and VI, without date and place of publication; Vol. VII, Leipzig, 1787.— August 25, 28, 1753.

ance from a German who was an authority on the drama and
who had collaborated on a theatrical publication with the
man who was to become *"der erste besonnene Herold Shake-
speares."* Alas, he is almost as severe on *Romeo and Juliet*[58]
as was Samuel Pepys himself, who considered it the worst
play he ever heard in his life:[59]

> I went to the theater in Covent Garden. Shakespeare's
> *Romeo and Juliet* was given. This merry tragedy, very
> faulty both in form and content (although it is seriously
> considered a real tragedy here), was performed accord-
> ing to its merits. Most of the actors, including Mr. Barry
> and Miss Rossiter, who are supposed to be the best,
> played with arrogant pomposity (*recht reibhandisch-
> heldenactionsmässig*). The newly added scene, the burial
> of Juliet,[60] is stupid and ridiculous. A bell is actually
> tolled on the stage. The costumes are mediocre and the
> decorations positively bad. . . . This disgusting piece is
> so well received here that it has had to be performed at
> least fourteen times in the last four weeks.

How much more interesting a review of this performance
would be if it came from Mylius' cousin and fellow reformer
of the German drama!

The next play which Mylius saw (November 14, 1753),
Ben Jonson's *Volpone,* was more to his liking. In fact, he
thought it might pass on the French or German stage, if
"a few necessary alterations" were made in the text. Just
one hundred and seventy-three years after Mylius made this
suggestion, *Volpone* was successfully produced in Berlin in
Stefan Zweig's version, but it is doubtful if the alterations
made therein were such as Mylius had in mind. The acting,
too, was more pleasing to Mylius in *Volpone* than in *Romeo
and Juliet,* though it was still *zu affectirt und reibhandisch.*
The afterpiece, however, Theobald's *Harlequin a Sorcerer,*

---

[58] *Tagebuch,* October 23, 1753.
[59] Pepys' *Diary,* March 1, 1662.
[60] M. is confused as to Garrick's alteration of Shakespeare's text at this
point. It consists chiefly in Juliet's awakening after Romeo has taken the
poison but before he dies.

a pantomime, was "absolutely beautiful."[61] The rapid and skilful shifting of scenes was quite impressive. Typical of English freedom was a scene showing the equestrian statue of George I, but with Harlequin seated upon it instead of the King. Where but in England, the German spectator must have asked himself, could such liberties be taken with royalty, living or dead?

Mylius saw Glover's *Boadicea* at Drury Lane on December 7, six days after its première.[62] This blank-verse tragedy was conventional and bombastic enough to win the full approval of the Continental critic, who had graduated from the school of Gottsched to that of Voltaire. He pronounced it not only the most "regular" English tragedy, but the best, despite its one great fault, the total lack of intrigue, a deficiency largely offset by "the beauty of the characters, emotions and sentiments." Garrick, Mrs. Pritchard and Mrs. Cibber receive some praise for their acting, though they are still somewhat *reibhandisch*. The incidental music by Dr. Boyce was very pretty. So great was Mylius' admiration for this drama that he wrote to Mr. Glover "on occasion of his new tragedy *Boadicea*" a letter which he signed "Christl. Mills" and which "a Scotchman, Mr. Maclean,"[63] translated into English for him.[64]

Hoadly's *The suspicious Husband* is in Mylius' opinion an excellent comedy despite "the curious entrances and exits of the characters and the irregular changes of scene."[65] As for Garrick in the rôle of Ranger, he is pronounced unsurpassable. Evidently he was not so *reibhandisch* as usual, or Mylius was cultivating a taste for English acting. From now on "the English Roscius" looms large in German discussions of the London stage. His greatness is proclaimed in the German

---

[61] In his *Der Kuss,* M. gave the leading rôle to Harlequin, in defiance of Gottsched.

[62] See Nicoll, A., *A History of late 18th Century Drama,* Cambridge University Press, 1927, p. 265.

[63] Probably Charles Macklin, the actor-playwright.

[64] *Tagebuch,* January 11, 1754.

[65] *ibid.,* November 17, 1753.

classic of dramatic criticism, Lessing's *Hamburgische Dramaturgie*, and in many other contemporary German works. The Italian operas which Mylius heard, Pasticcio's *Nerone* (November 20), Vanneschi and Galuppi's *Enrico* (December 1), and Giordani and Cocchi's *Gli Amanti gelosi* (December 31), made no deep impression upon him. At the last performance he attended, on December 31, he was again shocked by the irreverence of the British. When the King and Princess Amalia arrived, the people showed "their ill-bred pleasure by boisterous applause and shouting" and even dared to demand *encores* without consulting the pleasure of His Majesty.

In 1757 another friend of Lessing, Johann Joachim Ewald (1727-1811), spent five months in England. In letters to Kleist, Ramler, Gleim, Nicolai and von Brandt he expressed his unbounded admiration for everything English. The friends of the deceased poet Thomson, whose *Seasons* Ewald had translated into German,[66] became his "bosom friends," and John Shebbeare, whom he acclaims as the greatest living English genius, was especially dear to him. Ewald evidently continued to thrive in England on the same species of sentimental friendship to which he had been accustomed at home. His attachment to English institutions extended to the theaters, which he visited along with other places of interest, but he has nothing to say about the performances which he witnessed.[67]

Johann Peter Willebrand (1719-1786), a native of Rostock and a jurist of Altona, shared to a limited degree Ewald's enthusiasm for England, but seems to have had none of Ewald's capacity for friendship, for he laments that he has succeeded in the whole course of his life in winning but one

[66] According to the article on Ewald in the *A.D.B.*; a translation of *The Seasons* by Ewald is not listed in L. M. and M. B. Price, *The Publication of English Literature in Germany.*

[67] For Ewald's impressions of England see his *Briefe an Ramler* in *Archiv für Litteraturgeschichte*, Leipzig, 1875, Vol. IV, pp. 281-9; *Briefe an Kleist, ibid.*, pp. 445-52; *Bisher ungedruckte Briefe an von Brandt, Gleim und Nicolai, ibid.*, Vol. XIII, pp. 448-84; Vol. XIV, pp. 250-80.

true friend, and that one only with the "bitterest pains."[68]
Willebrand is quite matter-of-fact, another forerunner of
Baedeker, but his naïveté adds a touch of interest now and
then to his usually dry pages. He addresses his remarks to
young men with *Wanderlust* and advises them to equip themselves for their travels with health, money, attentiveness,
patience, piety, Latin, French and Italian. He draws up a
"general instruction," composed of fifty-two rules for tourists, with a long supplementary list intended especially for
university students. He is an avowed enemy of discursive
scribbling (*weitläuftige Schreiberei*), contenting himself with
tables and outlines. Included among the places of interest in
London are "das Opernhaus auf dem Haymarket" and "die
Comödie in Drury Lane," but there is no intimation as to what
may be seen within these houses. Nothing more is to be
learned from Willebrand about the theaters save the price
of admission.

The coronation of a Hanoverian king naturally attracted
German noblemen to England. Among those who crossed the
Channel in 1761 to attend the coronation of George III and
Queen Charlotte, Princess of Mecklenburg-Strelitz, was
Friedrich Graf von Kielmannsegge, whose diary has been
preserved, though it remained in manuscript for nearly a century and a half.[69] Count Kielmannsegge was a cousin of Sir
William Howe, commander of the British forces in America,
1776-1778, and was quite at home in England.[70] During this
visit of seven months he frequently attended the theaters and
usually wrote something of his impressions in his diary. It

[68] *Historische Berichte und practische Anmerkungen auf Reisen in
Deutschland,* neue vermehrte und verbesserte Auflage, Leipzig, 1769 (1st
ed. 1758) ; see p. 26.

[69] *Diary of a Journey to England in the Years 1761-1762,* trans. (from
the MS.) by Countess Kielmannsegg, London, New York, and Bombay,
1902.

[70] He was also related to the poet Platen and to Christian Albrecht von
Kielmannsegge (1748-1811), friend of Jerusalem (Werther) and a mem-
ber of Goethe's Wetzlar circle. See Eduard Graf von Kielmannsegg's
Familien-Chronik der Herren, Freiherren und Grafen von Kielmannsegg,
Leipzig und Wien, 1872, pp. 26, 423, 426, 467.

was a good season for Shakespeare. The count saw two performances of *Richard III* in Cibber's version, two of *Cymbeline*; and *Hamlet, King Lear, Romeo and Juliet* and *Henry
VIII*; also the "Coronation" from *Henry VIII* as an afterpiece. He mentions no tragedies except Shakespeare's, but he
saw many comedies, including Cibber's *The careless Husband,* in which he especially admired O'Brien as Lord Fop-
pington and Mrs. Clive as the soubrette;[71] Farquhar's *The
Beaux' Stratagem* with Garrick as Scrubb;[72] Jonson's *Every
Man in his Humour,* Beaumont and Fletcher's *Rule a Wife
and have a Wife,*[73] Murphy's *The Way to keep Him,*[74] and
the same author's *All in the Wrong,* which, to Kielmannsegge's satisfaction, "is quite like a French play"; and Jonson's *The Alchemist.* He also mentions a number of afterpieces of various types, the first of them being *Polly Honey-
combe,* by George Colman the elder, in which "Miss Pope
distinguished herself."[75] But this satirical skit was performed
so often that it became wearisome.[76] Kielmannsegge was also
an enthusiastic opera-goer and frequently comments on the
performances.

It is the acting rather than the plays that appeals to Kielmannsegge in London. His predilection for French classicism
is apparent now and then, as, for instance, when he says of
King Lear, which he prefers in Garrick's subdued version:[77]

> This play is very much in the style of the old English plays
> which were in fashion when the author wrote it, in which
> most of the characters go mad or get blind, or die; but
> as the English taste has changed latterly, many altera-
> tions have been made in this tragedy; amongst others
> the omission of the court jester, who in the original
> brings his tomfooleries in everywhere, even in the most
> tragic scenes.

[71] *Diary,* p. 25.
[72] *ibid.,* p. 26.
[73] *ibid.,* p. 209.
[74] *ibid.,* p. 212.
[75] *ibid.,* p. 26.
[76] *ibid.,* pp. 39, 82, 212, 214.
[77] *ibid.,* p. 214.

The funeral scene in *Romeo and Juliet* strikes him very much as it did Mylius. It seems "rather profane," with the bells tolling and the choir singing. But Kielmannsegge, unlike Mylius, thinks, "putting this aside, nothing could be presented more beautifully or naturally."[78] Only once does he find fault with English acting. The first time he saw *Richard III* he considered all the actors "indifferent or bad" except Holland as Richard and Mrs. Pritchard as Elizabeth, the queen mother.[79] It was probably expressly to see Garrick in the title-rôle that Kielmannsegge went to the play again. After his second theater evening he concluded that the English stage in general "has a good cast for every piece; and the faces of the actors look as if they were cut out for the characters which they represent."[80] His admiration for the acting increased as he saw more of it. He is soon convinced "that there is no theater in the world which equals the English in its choice of actors; at Drury Lane, for example, you have the impression that every actor has been expressly made for his part."[81] Later on he reaffirms that "the English stage has no superior in the world";[82] on it "everything is produced with the highest degree of truth. This effect can be obtained more easily here than upon any other stage, owing to the quantity of actors, including dancers and singers, of whom fifty are sometimes to be seen on one night, whilst there are probably as many absent, and the quantity of different decorations, machinery, and dresses, which are provided regardless of cost and with thorough completeness." His highest praise is naturally for Garrick,[83] "the only one who can delineate every character with equal skill, from the philosopher down to the fool, and who appears to put on a different face with each character."

[78] *Diary,* p. 221.
[79] *ibid.,* p. 39.
[80] *ibid.,* p. 26.
[81] *ibid.,* p. 192.
[82] *ibid.,* p. 221.
[83] *ibid.,* p. 192.

One of the most relentless and exhaustive German writers on foreign countries was Johann Jacob Volkmann (1732-1803). His books, though now very dull reading, were long useful guides for tourists. The first of them was devoted to Italy[84] and served Goethe as a guide on his Italian journey. After a long residence in Italy and France, Volkmann went in 1761 to the British Isles, accompanied by his brother. The result of this trip was four substantial volumes on England[85] and one on Scotland and Ireland.[86] Volkmann had acquired the language of the countries he was to visit as best he could in Leipzig and Göttingen, having given years to the task, and he travelled leisurely enough, spending, for instance, nineteen months in Paris. He was perhaps better prepared to acquaint his fellow countrymen with the outside world than any of his predecessors in the attempt, but his powers of observation were limited and his style is heavy. In the thousand pages which he wrote on England there is but little about the theaters.[87] No dramatic work is mentioned, and no dramatist except Shakespeare, "whose works are still quite popular." A footnote is devoted to Garrick's genius. Only one unfavorable comment is made on the English drama, namely that "the expression in English comedies is often too free, offending moral ears." The decorations are described as handsome and the costumes as gorgeous, being trimmed in some instances with genuine gold and silver.

The audiences must have been on their best behavior during the season of Kielmannsegge's and Volkmann's visits. The former only notes the persistent demands of gallery and pit for the singing of "God save great George, the King" on one occasion when the King and Queen were present;[88] and Volkmann even has a word of praise: "Much better order

---

[84] Three vols., 1770-1771.
[85] *Neueste Reisen durch England, vorzüglich in Absicht auf die Kunstsammlungen, Naturgeschichte, Oekonomie, Manufacturen und Landsitze der Grossen,* 4 vols., Leipzig, 1781-1783.
[86] 1784.
[87] *Neueste Reisen,* Vol. II, pp. 297ff.
[88] *Diary,* p. 225.

prevails in English theaters than in French and Italian. One usually listens quietly and attentively and refrains from applause or laughter until the actor reaches a pause. One does not join in humming the airs in the operettas as in Italy. Much less are the boxes turned into salons or reception rooms as is done by the Italian ladies, who with the buzz of their conversation make it almost impossible for the singers to be heard." Furthermore, "packing the house" is less common than in Paris or Venice.

While England's long period of European ascendancy in almost every field of human endeavor may be said to date from the treaty of Utrecht in 1715, it was not until past the middle of the century that Germany was awakened spiritually and became eagerly receptive of English influence. Though important beginnings had been made long before, it was left for the Seven Years' War to bind the two countries closely together by means of cultural as well as political ties. Even before Shakespeare's flame had begun to kindle the minds of certain German poets, three great vitalizing and democratizing currents had freely flowed from England into German literature. The moral weeklies of Steele and Addison soon bore fruit in Germany, beginning with the *Zuschauer,* which made its appearance in Hamburg in 1713, but two years after the launching of the *Spectator* in London. Many similar periodicals appeared throughout the first half of the century, with the *Discourse der Mahlern,* the organ of Bodmer and Breitinger in their controversy with Gottsched, as the most important. Then came the middle-class tragedy, when in 1755 Lessing's *Miss Sara Sampson* transplanted to German soil the new drama established largely by Lillo in his *George Barnwell*. Richardson's moralizing novels of family life soon followed, affecting other types of literature as well as the novel itself. But despite these and other literary importations from England, there is very little evidence that our German travellers in this early period were aware that German literature, after a century of sterility, was beginning to take on new life under English influence. Such an alert and gifted

young man as the poet Albrecht von Haller, for instance, even
after a visit to England, was ignorant of the fact that a great
literature was among the possessions of that country. Of
the travellers discussed above, only Pöllnitz and, curiously
enough, the Gottschedian Bielfeld, suggest by a syllable that
German dramatists had anything to learn from the English.
Pöllnitz holds that the French in their strict adherence to
fixed laws of dramatic composition are quite as much at fault
as the English in their extreme disregard of all rules, and
Bielfeld discovers that the license allowed in English comedy
makes for a degree of naturalness and liveliness unattainable
where exact rules hold sway. With the exception of these
heretical views, unquestioning belief in French classicism
still generally prevails. Doubtless because the rules and traditions accepted on the Continent were less rigid in comedy than
in tragedy, and deviation from the norm consequently less
startling, foreigners on the whole preferred English comedy
to English tragedy. Muralt, however, holds that the temperament of the people and the spirit of their language point to
the potential greatness of the English in the tragic genre. But
he was able to find only certain scattered passages in their
dramatic works which to his satisfaction bore out this opinion.
If he examined any particular drama as a whole, he found
it too contradictory to the rules, too much a hodgepodge of
tragedy and comedy, to be considered a real work of art.

All these early visitors to London were impressed by the
enthusiasm of the English people for theatrical performances,
and unlike other contemporary witnesses and later German
travellers, they are either silent or complimentary as to the
behavior of the audiences. The moralists among them, such
as Muralt and Alberti, are shocked by the vulgarity and indecency of the London stage, but all who express their
opinions on the subject, with the single exception of Mylius,
are favorably impressed by the staging and in general the
mechanical side of the productions. The acting also elicits
their praise. Alberti, Mylius and Kielmannsegge, at least, saw
the most illustrious of English actors, David Garrick.

CHAPTER II

RISE OF ANGLOMANIA

FEW Germans of his day became so imbued with the English spirit as the great Westphalian, Justus Möser (1720-1794). His interest in the English language and English literature was aroused in his youth by J. F. von dem Bussche, who through his travels was well acquainted with England and other foreign countries.[1] Möser went to London on a diplomatic mission in 1763 at the close of the Seven Years' War and remained there for eight months, devoting his spare time to a study of the constitution, politics, industry, commerce, literature, theaters and other public amusements, and the character of the English people. To this large task he brought a remarkably clear and penetrating mind, which enabled him to grasp certain phases of English culture as but few foreigners had. During the half century of his faithful legal and political service to his native Osnabrück, which in 1763 came under English rule, he was able to translate into realities many of the theories he had derived from English sources. It is a well known fact that Goethe learned his most valuable lessons in statesmanship from Möser and that he instigated the collection of Möser's scattered essays which were published as *Patriotische Phantasien* and to which such high tribute is paid in *Dichtung und Wahrheit*. The fact that Goethe looked to Möser as something of a literary as well as political authority is shown by his submitting his *Egmont* manuscript to Möser's criticism.[2]

Möser's most important works are his *Patriotische Phantasien* and his *Osnabrückische Geschichte,* both of which have

---

[1] Möser, J., *Sämmtliche Werke,* 10 vols., Berlin, 1843; see *Leben,* by Nicolai, Vol. X, p. 15.

[2] It has been supposed that the manuscript which Goethe submitted to Möser may have been *Iphigenie* instead of *Egmont.* But the very fact that the work in question was submitted to a critic who was primarily a statesman is strong evidence that it was *Egmont.*

an especial appeal to present-day Germany. But some of his best efforts were devoted to the reformation of the German stage. Originally adhering to Gottsched and the French school, he gradually shifted ground to become one of the chief opponents of pseudo-classicism and took a positive stand for realism and nationalism in drama. His first literary effort, *Arminius* (1748), a Gottschedian tragedy, is unimportant as a drama, but exceedingly important as an early experiment in dramatizing episodes from German history. Two decades later Möser was preaching the doctrine that orators, poets and writers should not merely aim at instruction and entertainment, but should dedicate their talents to the service of the state, and he points to England as the country in which "all satires, comedies, ethical doctrines (*Sittenlehren*), in fact, often sermons, are closely connected with the affairs of state."[3]

Möser was one of the earliest and ablest partisans of Lessing in his struggle against Gottsched and French influence. In 1761, just two years after Lessing had definitely sought in his famous seventeenth *Literaturbrief* to turn German writers from French to English models, Möser raised his voice to the same purpose in his *Harlequin, oder Verteidigung des Groteske-Komischen*.[4] His defense of English against French literary traditions takes the form of a plea for the clown, who had been banished by Gottsched; and, somewhat paradoxically, for the *commedia dell' arte* as a whole. The following sentences on the legitimate range of the theater could well have come from the pen of Lessing, but for their awkward style, which, for that matter, is far from characteristic of Möser:[5]

> The sphere of human enjoyment may be enlarged, and the peculiar spirit of the English has in our times found new and more varied perfections even in crooked lanes than in the eternally uniform and invariably straight

[3] *Werke,* Vol. III, p. 90.
[4] *ibid.,* Vol. IX, pp. 63-106.
[5] *ibid.,* p. 68.

promenades of which one may foresee at the very en-
trance the whole monotonous course, [one] always
has the end in view, and usually reaches it in a state
of supreme boredom. Nature is inexhaustible in figures
through which she lavishes her charms upon eager eyes,
and manners and passions are just as varied as human
faces.

In a similar vein he defends *The Beggar's Opera* and the
plays of Wycherly against the onslaught of the Abbé le
Blanc, who declared himself "amazed that honest people can
take pleasure in the society of beggars and highway robbers."
Möser prefers such company to the conventional world of the
Jesuit drama. In his opinion,[6] "a king is only too glad to descend from his throne for diversion, and everybody takes
a certain pleasure in leaving the beaten track."

Nicolai states that Möser sent him two plays of his own
composition from London, *Harlequin, ein Nachspiel,*[7] written as a specimen of the "grotesque-comic," illustrating the
author's theories; and a *"weinerliche Comödie"* entitled, according to Nicolai's recollection, *Isabella,* evidently based on
English models, which was lost through the carelessness of
the actor Döbbelin.[8] In a short essay written in 1773[9] Möser
says that he had selected twelve orphans ten years previously
and developed them into a company of actors. Apparently
nothing further is known of this scheme, but it was launched
immediately after Möser's return from England and attests
to his interest in the profession of acting. He undoubtedly
viewed with a critical eye the performance of English actors,
of whose accomplishments he had heard much. With all his
predilection for English drama, he found the London stage
of the time an unmitigated disappointment, perhaps, as he
says,[10] because his expectations had been too great. He recog-

[6] *Werke,* Vol. IX, p. 100.
[7] *ibid.,* pp. 107-36; English trans. by J. A. F. Wernecke, London, 1766,
dedicated to Garrick.
[8] *ibid.,* Vol. X, pp. 64, 137.
[9] *Nachricht einer einheimischen beständigen und wohlfeilen Schaubühne.*
[10] *Brief an Gleim,* 15. Dezember 1763, *Werke,* Vol. X, pp. 212ff.

nized the genius of Garrick, but knew him doubtless only by reputation. At any rate he wrote Gleim in December that he had been unable to see Garrick, as the latter was abroad.[11] It is evident that the great actor's fame was well known to Möser even before his visit to England, for in 1760 he addressed to Joseph Partridge a letter intended actually for Herzog Ferdinand von Braunschweig,[12] showing his familiarity with the famous passage in *Tom Jones* on Garrick's acting. In a long letter to Gleim on the theaters Möser expresses his surprise that there are only two houses besides the opera, far too few, in his opinion, for a city of the size of London. Even the *Beggar's Opera,* which he had previously defended sight unseen, seemed to him quite unworthy of the popularity it enjoyed. He was particularly disappointed in the performance of English tragedy. "The princesses are pretty little things, and the princes are quite undersized (*aus dem dritten Gliede*)." To meet with his approval, all tragic actors required the stature of Prussian grenadiers by way of compensation for the discarded cothurnus. European dress, the Spanish excepted, simply accentuated the physical insignificance of the actors. The action seemed more pompous than forceful. "Quiet grandeur" was unknown to the English stage. (It is evident that Möser's ideal of art, despite his sponsorship of the clown and his admiration of "crooked lanes," was still Winckelmann's "edle Einfalt und stille Grösse.") The actors "gesticulate incessantly with their hands like theological students in the pulpit, and scan their lines till one's ears ache." They sacrifice the spirit of the play as a whole to the effectiveness of certain telling passages. For example, if God had to show his divine wrath on the English stage, it would surely be by means of thunder and lightning. The comic performances were better, on the whole, but still fell far short of Möser's expectations. They had the advantage of a lively and

---

[11] Garrick was on the "Grand Tour" from September 15, 1763, to April 27, 1765; see Fitzgerald, P., *Life of David Garrick,* 2 vols., London, 1868, Vol. II, p. 113.

[12] *Werke,* Vol. IX, p. 55.

effective tempo, otherwise they were no better than similar performances elsewhere. Even Foote, the famous actor-playwright, was a disappointment, being "in one play precisely the same as in another, consequently no genius, but a carefully trained copyist." Not only the actors, however, but the repertoire as well failed to win Möser's approbation. "In all the time I have been here," he says quite unexpectedly, "I have not seen a single regular (*regelmässig*) piece performed." We might expect something different from the man who two years earlier had claimed to prefer the devious ways of English drama to the symmetrical avenues of the French. But, as in the case of Lessing, his dramatic theories were more advanced than his personal taste.

Möser was intimately acquainted with at least one English actor, the none too reputable Shuter.[13]

Another ally of Lessing in bringing the German theater into line with the English, and a more consistent one than Möser, was Helferich Peter Sturz (1736-1779). Like Möser, Sturz had prepared himself for the legal profession but cultivated at the same time his interest in literature and especially in the drama. From 1764 to 1772 Sturz was attached to the court of Christian VII of Denmark. In 1768 he visited London and Paris. His *Briefe*[14] describing the journey first appeared in the *Deutsches Museum,* and easily surpass, so far as they go, everything written on England by German visitors up to that time. In 1767 Sturz had published a middle-class tragedy, *Julie,*[15] one of the many imitations of Lessing's *Miss Sara Sampson.* Sturz' play, of which the plot is based on Frances Brooke's *Julia Mandeville,* is even more lachrymose than its famous German model. One of the characters, Julie's governess, is in fact aware that she is running the risk of weeping her eyes out.[16] Scenes from a *Medea* by

---

[13] *Werke,* Vol. I, p. 155.

[14] *Briefe, im Jahre 1768 auf einer Reise im Gefolge des Königs von Dänemark geschrieben.*

[15] *Julie, ein bürgerliches Trauerspiel in fünf Aufzügen, mit einem Briefe über das deutsche Theater,* Kopenhagen und Leipzig, 1767.

[16] Act II, scene I.

Sturz, probably suggested by the character of Marwood in
Miss Sara Sampson, are extant, and he also tried his hand at
translating English plays. A fragmentary rendition by Sturz
of Foote's *Mayor of Garret* was published in the *Deutsches
Museum,*[17] and the editor of his collected works remembered
having seen among his unfinished writings "a very happy
translation" of Colman and Garrick's *The clandestine Marriage.*[18]

Like Pöllnitz and Lessing, Sturz favors for the German
drama a middle course between English daring and French
timidity, and like Möser and Herder he directs German
dramatists to the history of their own country for source
material.

Sturz was an intimate friend of Klopstock. In 1767 he
made Lessing's acquaintance in Hamburg and formed a lasting friendship with him. Both he and Heinrich Füssli, the
next in order of our Germans in England, were friends of
Angelica Kaufmann in London. Accompanied by Colman,
Sturz visited Dr. Johnson, whom he calls "the colossus of
English literature," and forgetting that Johnson had edited
Shakespeare, asked him what was the best edition.[19] He also
knew Foote and Murphy and other English theater men, and
he and Garrick, if we may judge by the tone of their letters,
formed a warm mutual attachment. To Sturz, as to many
of his German contemporaries, English drama was Shakespeare and the English stage, Garrick. He hoped that Garrick's art might influence German acting, "now that Shakespeare and nature find more favor with us." In his first London letter[20] Sturz writes of Garrick the man, saying that he
will not speak for the moment of Garrick the actor. In a footnote added some years later, he says he has resolved never
to write on that subject, for nothing could be added to what
Lichtenberg had meanwhile said. But no resolution was

[17] 1779, Vol. II, pp. 19-31.
[18] See *Schriften,* 2 vols., Wien, 1819, Vol. I, p. xii.
[19] *Nachschrift, 3. Brief aus London,* Deutsches Museum, 1777, Vol. I,
p. 461; not included in *Schriften.*
[20] *Schriften,* Vol. I, pp. 100*ff.*

sufficient to suppress Sturz' praise of Garrick. Even in his
first letter he writes that a certain foreigner in his box, though
understanding not a word of English, was so moved by Garrick's mere gesture in reaching out for an imaginary dagger
in *Macbeth* that he collapsed in a swoon. To illustrate how
Garrick puts his whole soul into his art, he describes a re-
hearsal of Bickerstaffe's *The Padlock* which he attended:[21]

> He had no rôle in it himself, yet he acted all the parts,
> even the female rôles, with convincing realism, for the
> benefit of the cast. It is incomprehensible that his delicate
> nervous system can endure this constant strain, that his
> health does not succumb. For you are not to suppose that
> this storm is merely on the surface. I saw him once after
> he had finished playing the rôle of Richard reclining on
> a bench, like the dying Germanicus in Poussin's picture,
> with heaving breast, pale, covered with perspiration, his
> hands limp and quivering, speechless.

In a letter to Garrick from Paris[22] Sturz analyzes Mlle.
Clairon's acting. Much as he admires her skill, he senses that
"this portrayer of all feelings herself feels but little"; every
movement is studied, every expression predetermined. To
him French acting in general seems conventional, standard-
ized and affected, but he bears in mind differences in national
taste and aligns Germany more definitely with England in
this respect than even Lessing had up to that time:[23] "To be
sure, judged by Northern taste, they [the French] exaggerate pose, gait and declamation, . . . however, they are acting not for us but for their fellow-countrymen." Garrick's
reply to this letter, very cordial in tone, sums up Sturz' own
thoughts:[24]

> Your idea of the French most exactly agrees with mine;
> their politeness has reduced their character to such same-

[21] *Schriften*, Vol. I, p. 106.
[22] *ibid.*, pp. 182–98.
[23] *ibid.*, p. 198.
[24] *ibid.*, p. 199. This letter is quoted in *David Garrick and his French
Friends* (New York, *ca.* 1911, pp. 243f.), by Frank A. Hedgcock, who says,
"It was written to a Danish friend, Mr. Sturtz."

ness; their humours and passions are so curbed by habit, that when you have seen a half dozen French men and women, you have seen the whole; in England every man is a distinct being, and requires a distinct study to investigate him. It is from this great variety that our comedies are less uniform than the French, and our characters more strong and dramatic.

In his *Nachrichten von Samuel Foote*[25] Sturz eulogizes the great caricaturist both as a personality and in his restricted field as an actor. Sturz' early death removed one of the most important links connecting the literary world of Germany with that of England.

Johann Heinrich Füssli (1741-1825) can hardly be called a visitor to England, for he took up his abode there in 1763, and as Henry Fuseli became the foremost English artist of his day with the exception of Reynolds and West. The most noted member of a Zürich family of scholars and artists, he was a godson of Salomon Gessner, a pupil of Bodmer and Breitinger at the Collegium Carolinum in Zürich, and a friend of Lavater, who dedicated to him a volume which he translated into English as *Aphorisms on Man*. As a student at Zürich he became enamoured of Shakespeare and undertook a translation of *Macbeth* into German. For the Shakespeare Gallery started by Boydell in 1786 Füssli supplied a number of paintings, especially of scenes from *Hamlet, Macbeth* and *King Lear*. John Knowles in his *Life and Writings of Henry Fuseli*[26] tells of the artist's admiration for Garrick's acting:

At this time Garrick was in the height of his reputation; and as Fuseli considered the theater the best school for a foreigner to acquire the pronunciation of the English language, and Garrick's performance an excellent imitation of the passions, which would give him a lesson essential to historical designs: he never missed the opportunity of seeing him act, and he was generally found in the front row of the pit: to obtain which, he often used much

[25] *Schriften,* Vol. II, pp. 181-212.
[26] Three vols., London, 1831; see Vol. I, p. 39.

personal exertion, and put himself in positions of hazard and inconvenience. And he has often dwelt with delight upon the performances of the man who represented so well the stormy passions of Richard, or the easy libertinism of Ranger [in *The suspicious Husband*]; and then could descend to the credulous Abel Drugger [in *The Alchemist*], and in the character of the silly tobacconist, so alter the expression of his countenance as scarcely to be recognized as the person who had delineated the high character in the historic art.

Füssli also admired Kean in certain rôles, especially as Shylock, but he thought that this actor erred in undertaking parts that were beyond him, as for instance, that of Orestes; and as for Mrs. West in the rôle of Hermione, he said in a letter to a friend:[27] "She was well dressed, and has a good voice, but no use of it, and tore her part to tatters in one long uninterrupted fit of raving." Füssli, if his biographer paints an authentic picture of him, was virtually made over into an Englishman.

With the exception of such men as Füssli and George Forster, who is to be included later, to both of whom England became a second fatherland, none of our German travellers felt more at home on English soil than did Georg Christoph Lichtenberg (1742-1799), the distinguished Göttingen scholar.[28] Lichtenberg is known in the history of physics as the inventor of the "Lichtenberg figures," but he is even more important as a man of letters than as a scientist. He is the greatest German satirist before Heine, and it is in the satirical vein especially that he shows his English proclivities. With Sturz he was the chief opponent of the Sterne cult in Germany,[29] and he likewise opposed the whole sentimental tendency embodied in the *Göttinger Hainbund*. To counteract such currents in contemporary literature,

---

[27] Knowles' *Life*, Vol. I, p. 378.

[28] cf. Mattheson, P. E., *German Visitors to England, 1770-1795*, Taylorian Lecture, Oxford University Press, 1930. Mattheson discusses also Moritz, Archenholz and Wendeborn.

[29] See Thayer, H. W., *Laurence Sterne in Germany*, New York, Columbia University Press, 1905, pp. 158, 160.

he established with George Forster in 1780 the *Göttingsche Magazin*. In 1794 he began to issue his explanations of Hogarth's engravings, which won for him lasting fame. His most important literary work, however, is his aphorisms.

Lichtenberg first visited England for a few weeks in 1770; he returned in September 1774, this time remaining fifteen months. Like Goethe in Rome and like Heinrich Heine when newly arrived in Paris, Lichtenberg felt that in London he was in his natural element. His position at court, secured by the scientific mission in which he was engaged, and his cordial relations with the King and Queen, gave him ready access to the leading social and intellectual circles. Furthermore, his command of the English language was excellent; in fact, he proudly informs his closest friend, the Göttingen book-dealer Johann Christian Dieterich, that Garrick had declared his English to be the best he had ever heard a foreigner speak.[30]

While many scattered comments on England and Englishmen are to be found in Lichtenberg's letters and other writings, it is only of the theater and more particularly of Garrick's acting that he wrote at all comprehensively, and even his *Briefe aus London,* which are devoted exclusively to dramatic criticism, give by no means a systematic exposition of his views. In fact, he writes in an informal, almost haphazard manner, declaring that he "detests nothing more than Boswellian bombast and pompousness, and the prophetic tone." The letters were written at the request of Christian Heinrich Boie, who was especially active in purveying English culture to Germany, and appeared in the *Deutsches Museum,* of which Boie was editor.[31]

Of the repertoire of the English stage Lichtenberg has practically nothing to say. Between the composition of Sturz' *Letters* and his own, the *Hamburgische Dramaturgie* and

[30] *Briefe,* hrsg. von A. Leitzmann & C. Schüddekopf, 3 vols., Leipzig, 1901; see Vol. I, p. 240.

[31] June, November, 1776; January, May, 1778. German visitors to England who contributed to Boie's periodical included also Archenholz, Büsch, Fabricius and Cordes.

Von deutscher Art und Kunst had appeared, and English drama through its greatest representative had won out for all time in Germany. The day when a German scholar could speak of "the famous Shakespeare" in some empty phrase borrowed from a history of English literature was past. While the chief credit for the acceptance of Shakespeare and English drama is properly ascribed to Lessing and Herder, some recognition must also be given to Möser and Sturz and other visitors to England, even to the modest intercession of a Pöllnitz. Three Englishmen made the deepest impression on Lichtenberg and seemed to him to be closely akin to one another in spirit—Shakespeare, Hogarth and Garrick.[32] Just below this great triumvirate stood Fielding, who naturally appealed the more strongly to Lichtenberg for his opposition to Shandeism. On his second trip to England Lichtenberg visited Shakespeare's birthplace and wrote to Dieterich:[33]

> I have seen his house and sat in his chair, from which people have begun to cut pieces. I too cut off a shilling's worth of it. I shall have it set in rings for distribution among the *Jacobiten* and *Göthiter,* à la Lorenzo-snuff-boxes.[34]

He defends Shakespeare almost as a matter of course against Voltaire, taking a stand which a generation earlier would have rendered him ridiculous.[35] He has seen Mrs. Smith as Ophelia. Though not a remarkable actress, she is a great success in this rôle on account of her ability as a singer. "If Voltaire had only been here and heard Mrs. Smith as a Shakespeare commentator, I am inclined to think that the

---

[32] *Deutsches Museum,* June 1776, p. 567.

[33] *Briefe,* Vol. I, p. 240; October 17, 1775.

[34] A thrust at the Sterne cult in Germany, of which J. G. Jacobi was the leader. Lichtenberg is scarcely justified, however, in attacking Goethe on this score. Jacobi, touched by the exchange of snuff-boxes between the English traveller and the Franciscan monk Lorenzo in the *Sentimental Journey* adopted the snuff-box as a symbol of goodwill, and as such it was widely employed in the Gleim circle. See Martin, Ernst, *Ungedruckte Briefe von und an Johann Georg Jacobi,* Strassburg, 1874, pp. 10, 11, 12, 27, 52; cf. Thayer, H. W., *op. cit.,* pp. 84f.

[35] *D.M.,* November 1776, p. 987.

remarkable man would have regretted what he has said against these scenes." At any rate, were he, Lichtenberg, in Voltaire's place, he would apologize to Shakespeare's ghost. He observes with regret that Voltaire has gained at least one victory in Drury Lane, for the grave-diggers' scene is now omitted on that stage. And this omission provokes the one unfavorable comment on Garrick; he should never have suppressed this scene. As a true admirer of Shakespeare, Lichtenberg has no patience with the German *Genies* who fain would imitate him by the exact reproduction of nature and by general disorderliness and irregularity. In the course of his letters he makes a number of side thrusts at the *Stürmer und Dränger* in the spirit of Herder's remonstrances with Goethe over *Götz von Berlichingen,* and again and again he expresses his disapproval of French classicism.

Lichtenberg condemns one play, Vanbrugh's *Provok'd Wife,* on moral grounds. Although it has been toned down somewhat and at least represents the clergy in a more favorable light than originally, it still contains some disgusting scenes, offensive to eye and ear, he holds, and should be dropped from the repertoire.[36] Nor did he care for Shadwell's *The fair Quaker of Deal,* which he saw soon after his arrival in London, though he considered a few scenes in it very good, and was favorably impressed by the acting of Weston and Moody even in such an imperfect vehicle.[37]

Garrick never had a more enthusiastic follower than Lichtenberg. The well known *Briefe aus London,* which need not be summarized here,[38] are one long eulogy of the "English Roscius." Lichtenberg states in his first letter to Boie that he has seen Garrick eight times, and in the following rôles :

[36] *D.M.,* November 1776, p. 990; cf. *Brief an Baldinger,* January 10, 1775.

[37] *Briefe,* Vol. I, p. 195.

[38] See Betz, G., *Lichtenberg as a Critic of the English Stage,* Journal of English and Germanic Philology, Vol. XXIII, 1924, for an analysis of Lichtenberg's criticism and a discussion of its influence on Brockmann and probable influence on Schröder in their performances of the Hamlet rôle.

Abel Drugger in *The Alchemist,* Archer in *The Beaux' Stratagem,* Sir John Brute in *The provok'd Wife,* twice as Hamlet; as Lusignan in Hill's version of Voltaire's *Zaïre;* Benedick in *Much Ado about Nothing;* and Don Leon in *Rule a Wife and have a Wife.* He was introduced to Garrick on October 15, 1775, immediately before the performance of *As you like it,* and sat with Mrs. Garrick in her box, to which he thenceforth had free access,[39] presumably because he was contributing dramatic criticisms to a German periodical. There is no evidence, however, that he became well acquainted with Garrick personally. Moreover, his stay in London continued but a few weeks longer. So great was his enthusiasm that on one occasion he travelled some twenty-five English miles and fasted fourteen hours to see Garrick perform.[40] He offers the following explanation of Garrick's greatness:[41]

> He attended the school to which Shakespeare went, where he too, like the latter, instead of waiting for revelations, studied; for in England genius does not do everything, as is the case in Germany. I refer to London, where a man with such talent for observation may in one year easily bring the lessons which experience has taught him to a degree of perfection for which a whole life-time would not suffice in a town where everybody has the same hopes and fears, the same interests and enthusiasms, and where all things are uniform.

Lichtenberg only wonders that the varied life of London has not produced more Garricks, Hogarths and Fieldings. Yet Garrick strikes him as anything but a typical product of that city. "There is in his whole figure, movement and bearing," he says,[42] "something that I have found to a certain degree a few times among the few Frenchmen I have seen, but not at all among the many Englishmen I have known."

Lichtenberg analyzes in detail Garrick's representation of

[39] *Briefe,* Vol. I, p. 240.
[40] *D.M.,* May 1778, p. 23.
[41] *ibid.,* June 1776, p. 570.
[42] *ibid.,* p. 568.

Hamlet, Sir John Brute and Archer. The following passage is a specimen of his manner:[43]

> Of the phrase, "so excellent a king," the last word is suppressed; it is merely suggested by the movement of the mouth, which is then closed at once, quivering but firm, so that anguish which might not seem altogether manly may not be too plainly expressed by the lips.

In reply to an inquiry from Boie, real or imagined, as to whether he had been able to find no fault with Garrick's acting, our critic admitted that he had.[44] There had been one imperfect line in his Hamlet: "That one may smile, and smile, and be a villain"; which the actor repeated in a manner to suggest that he was the smiling villain himself. But this line was corrected and given as it should be in the second *Hamlet* performance which Lichtenberg attended!

Garrick's enemies claimed that Quin had equalled him as Sir John Brute and that Weston was his equal as Abel Drugger. As for Quin, never having seen him, Lichtenberg is not prepared to speak. But he observes that Quin's partisans say that he was himself a Sir John Brute; consequently it was no triumph for his art if he acted that part well. Nor did he see Weston as Abel Drugger, but, having seen him in other rôles, he considered it absurd to compare him with Garrick. Weston, to be sure, was a born comedian and had provoked him to laughter more than all other English actors combined, but Weston, like Quin, was brilliant only in certain congenial rôles. When he appeared, the greater part of the audience would forget the play for his sake and merely watch him do his antics, whereas Garrick's rôle was always the effective part of a whole, to which it was skilfully adjusted.[45] Superb were the scenes in *The Beaux' Stratagem,* familiar from Hogarth's engravings, in which Garrick and Weston appeared together.[46] Apparently Lichtenberg belonged to the larger part

[43] *D.M.,* November 1776, p. 985.
[44] *ibid.,* May 1778, p. 23.
[45] *ibid.,* June 1776, pp. 564f.
[46] *ibid.,* May 1778, p. 19; cf. *Brief an Baldinger,* January 10, 1775.

of the audience for whom the mere appearance of Weston
was sufficient. He liked him well enough in Henry Bate's *The
rival Candidates* to see him in that play a second time,[47] and
he was especially delighted with his portrayal of the servant
Hurry, a rôle devised for him in *The Maid of the Oaks,* "a
piece based on a true story and written by General Burgoyne
in honor of his niece, Lady Derby." "Probably few pieces in
the world have been performed with such tasteful magnificence and with such perfection as this," he adds; "the decorations were painted by Lutherburg and cost 10,000 Taler."[48]
He concludes an account of Weston's performance with an
explanation of the success of the play: "To him, Mrs. Abington and Mr. Dodd and the unusually magnificent decorations
is due the fact that this piece was performed twenty-three
times at the beginning of this year." To Baldinger he wrote[49]
that without Weston and Mrs. Abington *The Maid of the
Oaks* would scarcely have survived the first presentation. The
acting of Macklin also found high favor with this German
critic. Macklin's Shylock was deservedly second only to
Garrick's Hamlet as an attraction to London theater-goers.
Lichtenberg saw Macklin in his first performance of this rôle
after his lawsuit and was deeply stirred by his acting.[50] The
afterpiece, Macklin's *Love à la Mode,* in which the author
played the part of Sir Archy MacSarcasm, likewise won
Lichtenberg's praise. He also saw Macklin as Macbeth, "in
the same rôle which caused the disturbance leading to the

[47] *D.M.,* May 1778, p. 20.

[48] The decorations were painted by Philippe Jacques de Loutherbourg
(1740-1812), a native of Fulda, who was reared in Alsace and went to
London in 1771, where he promptly became Garrick's scenic designer; he
had an important influence on the staging of plays. Cf. W. J. Lawrence in
Johnson's England, ed. by A. S. Turberville, 2 vols., Oxford University
Press, 1933, Vol. II, pp. 185*f.*

[49] January 10, 1775.

[50] May 18, 1775; Macklin instigated the suit against Colman, manager of
Drury Lane, to recover damages for his dismissal from the cast of *The
Merchant of Venice* on the grounds, advanced by the public, that the Shylock rôle belonged exclusively to Smith, who for twenty years had been
the mainstay of the theater in tragedy.

suit,"[51] but this time his acting was marred by the handicap of advanced age.

The greatest actresses on the London stage were in Lichtenberg's opinion Mrs. Abington, Mrs. Barry, Mrs. Yates, and Mrs. Pope. Concerning Mrs. Abington he feels he could write a whole volume and yet fail to do justice to the subject, especially since it is more difficult to convey an impression of comic than of tragic acting.[52] He considers her the intellectual superior of all other English actresses and in her field as great as Mrs. Barry and Mrs. Yates in theirs. He gives a full description of her, not omitting details as to her dress, which set the fashion of the day. For these points he modestly admits that he relied on female guidance. He saw her in many different rôles and liked her best in *The provok'd Wife, The Beaux' Stratagem,* in Colman and Garrick's *Bon Ton,* in *Much Ado about Nothing,* and the *Maid of the Oaks.* Once at the opera he happened to be seated beside her and had the pleasure of lending her his libretto and exchanging a few casual remarks with her, all of which agitated him greatly, evoking the philosophical observation: "What acquaintances one does make when one travels!" But while this celebrated actress could portray only the *grande dame* in high comedy, Mrs. Barry was surpassed in versatility by Garrick alone. She was a real beauty, of the madonna type, and a born actress. On his first trip to England Lichtenberg saw her as Desdemona,[53] an unforgettable experience; and still more impressive was her portrayal of Cordelia in *King Lear,* "the greatest thing of the kind" he had ever seen.

Lichtenberg makes some interesting comments on historical accuracy in costume, called forth by current criticism of Garrick for appearing in French attire. Here again the great actor finds an ardent protagonist in his German critic, who admires him for not being too pedantic.

[51] *D.M.,* May 1778, p. 443. Lichtenberg is mistaken on this point. See preceding note.
[52] *ibid.,* pp. 435ff.
[53] *Brief an Baldinger,* January 10, 1775.

On the opera Lichtenberg has but little to say. He mentions having seen *The Beggar's Opera*,[54] but, strangely enough, makes no comment on it. He had looked forward eagerly to hearing Gabrielli sing, and finally realized his wishes on November 11, 1775, only after her performance had been cancelled three successive times: "Signora had *influenza,* as a cold in the head was called in London in those Italian days." He acknowledges that he is not a competent critic of operatic music, but confesses that he was grievously bored on this occasion. To be sure, some of the prima donna's arias were pleasing, but she was no actress at all, and the facial contortions accompanying her singing were horrible. Some compensation for these annoyances was afforded by the *danseuse* Barelli; but Professor Lichtenberg preferred a few minutes at Drury Lane to a whole evening at the Haymarket.[55]

His great admiration for the London stage did not blind this critic to the merits of German actors:[56] "Among those I have seen in Göttingen, Hannover and Hamburg . . . many could hold their own in Drury Lane, and a few would even create a sensation." Smith, Garrick's understudy, is pronounced far inferior to Eckhof. In his private correspondence Lichtenberg expresses himself more frankly on this point,[57] and, quite naturally, on others, declaring that if he had the means, he would load all the German actresses of his acquaintance on a ship and convey them to London so that they might learn from Mrs. Barry how to use their arms.

Of all German writers on the English theater of the eighteenth century Lichtenberg is the ablest.

It was probably Johann Wilhelm von Archenholz (1743-1812) who did most in his century to present a complete picture of England to the German public. As a youth of seventeen Archenholz entered the service of Frederick the Great, retiring at the end of the Seven Years' War with the rank of captain and a somewhat dubious reputation. He spent the

54 *Briefe,* Vol. I, p. 195.
55 *D.M.,* May 1778, pp. 439*f*.
56 *ibid.,* June 1776, p. 573.
57 *Brief an Baldinger,* January 10, 1775.

next fifteen years in travel and study in Germany, Holland,
Italy, France and England, investigating the history, government, politics and national characteristics of the different
countries. In 1780 he returned to Germany and entered upon
his busy career as a writer. Only one of his works is well
known in modern times, his *Geschichte des Siebenjährigen
Krieges,* which Carlyle used as a source of his *Frederick the
Great* and which in 1911 reached its eleventh edition. Another
of his more important works is his *Geschichte der Königin
Elisabeth.* He launched in 1781 a periodical, *Litteratur- und
Völkerkunde,* the first of a number of journalistic publications which continued until his death and which were chiefly
concerned with Great Britain. For a quarter of a century the
German view of England was derived more largely from
Archenholz than from any other single source. During the
earlier part of this period his almost unqualified admiration
for everything English contributed substantially to the rise
of anglomania in Germany. The French Revolution and its
repercussions abroad caused an almost complete reversal in
Archenholz' attitude towards the British nation; but his later
articles were not so widely read as his first systematic work,
England und Italien, which appeared in 1785 with a dedica-
tion to Wieland. It was soon translated into French, and a
translation from the French version of the part dealing with
England appeared in London in 1789.[58] With his mental
alertness, his keen powers of observation, and his pleasing
style, the author was well equipped to interpret foreign civi-
lizations to his fellow countrymen; but his strong personal
bias frequently militates against his objectivity. He repeatedly compares France and Italy with England, to the almost
invariable advantage of the northern nation. As for Italy, in
fact, his impressions seem to have been scarcely more favorable than those of a more famous German visitor to Rome
in the year 1510. All the lights of his picture fall upon England and all the shadows upon Italy. Jagemann, the Weimar
librarian, attempted a defense of Italian culture against the

[58] *A Picture of England,* 2 vols. in one.

attack of Archenholz.[59] Goethe too had a very poor opinion of Archenholz' description of Italy, which he read on his Italian journey;[60] but as late as 1826 Heine considered him along with Göde the best guide on a trip to England,[61] although Heine's attitude towards England, and towards Italy as well, was very nearly the reverse of that of Archenholz.

Above everything else it is English liberty that appeals to Archenholz, based, as he sees it, upon the public law-courts, trial by jury, the *habeas corpus* act, parliamentary representation, and, most important of all, freedom of the press. While his attention is fixed chiefly upon politics, government, industry and commerce, the "admirable public spirit," a phrase which he is at a loss to translate into German, and all such phases of the national life, he also devotes some space to a discussion of science and literature. He was an indefatigable theatergoer and especially enjoyed the musical pantomimes frequently given as afterpieces, in which the most remarkable national events were dramatized, Sheridan, even, taking a hand in composing them. The foremost of these was *The Jubilee*, which was performed at Dury Lane ninety-seven times during the winter of 1769-1770.[62] Archenholz saw twenty-eight presentations of this piece without suffering the slightest boredom. If he is not mistaken, he says, "Garrick himself was the author" of this, "probably the most magnificent pantomime ever seen in Europe."[63] Few could have been in a better position than he, after his twenty-eighth view, to give an account of the pageant, and he does discuss it in detail. The Shakespeare Jubilee was celebrated at Stratford-on-Avon for three days in September 1769. Guests streamed in from all over England, and many of them were compelled to lodge in tents, as the accommodations of the town were alto-

[59] Jagemann, *Briefe über Italien*, 3 vols., 1778-1785.

[60] *Brief an Herder, Werke*, Weimar ed., 4, Vol. VIII, p. 74.

[61] Heine, *Sämtliche Werke*, Leipzig, 1914, Vol. V, pp. 4, 517.

[62] Archenholz says ninety-seven times; Elizabeth P. Stein, *Three Plays of David Garrick*, New York, 1926, p. 64, says, following Genest, "It was played to crowded houses for ninety-two consecutive nights."

[63] *England und Italien*, 2. Ausgabe, 5 vols., Carlsruhe, 1787; English theaters are discussed in Vol. III, pp. 150-200.

gether inadequate. For his afterpiece, *The Jubilee,* Garrick
devised a setting which represented the town of Stratford,
and against this background he produced a great variety of
scenes portraying events "which had actually taken place, or
could have occurred, during the Jubilee." Then came a masquerade in which appeared characters and incidents from
Shakespeare's plays. The pageant lasted an hour and a half,
and as Archenholz describes it was much more elaborate than
the printed text of the piece suggests. The Paris celebration
in 1774 in honor of Voltaire was "but a wretched imitation
of the Shakespeare Jubilee." Aside from this the only stage
scenes which Archenholz discusses are the entombment of
Juliet, which, unlike Mylius, he found most moving; the
church scene in Cumberland's *The Carmelite*; and the group
of "Women of the Town" in *The Beggar's Opera.* Scenes of
this sort were effectively produced only in London, he
claimed. Nowhere else in the world were plays staged with
such taste and magnificence, nowhere else were actors and
actresses so generously rewarded for their services and held
in such high social esteem. The golden age of the English
theater was during Garrick's last years, his ablest assistants
being Abington, Barry, Woodward and Weston. But the
death of all these stars except Mrs. Abington within one
year[64] marked the beginning of a decline. To some extent
Mrs. Siddons and Henderson were able to rehabilitate the
London stage; but Henderson's early death was a new blow
to the theatrical world. By 1787 Mrs. Siddons' fame had
reached a height of which even Garrick in his most brilliant
period could scarcely boast.

On one point this critic contradicts Lichtenberg. He gives
Mrs. Abington credit for great versatility, describing her as
the Mrs. Siddons of comedy. At the age of fifty-two Mrs.
Abington was able to represent spoiled children with perfect
success and was equally accomplished as a peasant girl and
as a lady of rank.

[64] Actually, 1776-1779.

An admirable feature of the London stage which Archenholz is the first German writer to stress is that the actors
memorize their parts thoroughly. He cannot say so much for
those of other countries.—The baneful influence of the *Englische Komödianten* may still have been partly accountable
for the frequently mentioned deficiency of German actors in
acquiring their rôles.—The absence of the souffleur-box also
meets with his approval. This contrivance was invented in
France and adopted in all other countries except England,
where the prompter stood behind the scenes, not repeating
the entire text, but coming to the aid of the performers whenever they showed the slightest uncertainty. In England the actors never ignored the gallery, an offense, to be sure, of which
they were seldom guilty in France, but sometimes in Italy,
and most often in Germany. Archenholz shares Lichtenberg's
high opinion of German acting. He considers Schröder the
greatest actor since Garrick, and decidedly the superior of
the famous French actor, Le Kain, whom he had seen in
many rôles. Like Sturz and Smollett, Archenholz was recon-
ciled to the French stage tradition as suitable to the French
temperament, but his own decided preference was for the
English theater. English actors, to be sure, were given to vio-
lence and sometimes exceeded the limits of propriety. Consequently they were often lacking in dignity in the delineation
of certain characters. When French classics were performed
in English translation, the male rôles were usually travestied,
while the female rôles fared somewhat better. It is a relief to
hear this critic find some fault with English acting.

The behavior of the audience was particularly interesting
to this sympathetic onlooker. The English theater public, he
maintained, was superior in decorum to that of France and,
still more, of Italy, where "it is customary to play cards in
the loges during the performance and where it is in poor taste
for ladies to pay attention to what takes place on the stage."
The English audience was completely absorbed in the play and
deeply moved by tragic scenes. As proof of this observation

the performance of Mrs. Bellamy in *Oedipus*[65] in 1775 is cited. The actress herself was overcome by a sense of tragedy and had to be carried off the stage unconscious. And the audience, too, unable to endure the strain, departed, so that the piece had to be finished without the leading lady, before a handful of unusually hard-boiled spectators. But the audience, however afflicted by the tragic scenes, had its moments of hilarity :

> The uproar of the common people in the theater before the curtain rises is simply frightful. A foreigner, unfamiliar with such outbursts of freedom, imagines he is facing a field of battle on which the combatants are ready to break one another's necks. But fights are extremely rare. The common people in the galleries, where the din is greatest, are simply bent on making a noise to pass the time, and since several hundred people are crowded together who have no conception of decorum, but so much the more of personal liberty, the disorder is only natural. Before going to the theater, one fills one's pockets with oranges, which serve the double purpose of refreshment and entertainment. . . . But the peels are often hurled by the occupants of the gallery into the pit, or they land there if they miss the proscenium, at which they are usually aimed. . . . They are so heaped up by the time for the curtain to rise that a servant must enter with a broom. But when the play begins, all noise and bombardment ceases, unless some especial provocation gives rise to further disturbances; and one is bound to admire the quiet attentiveness of such an estimable folk.

On one evening Archenholz witnessed a stirring scene at Drury Lane when an unsuccessful attempt was made to perform Hugh Kelly's *A Word to the Wise*. The author, a personal friend of Garrick, had shifted from the people's cause to that of the ministry, having employed his pen on each side in turn. Consequently the people refused to give his play a hearing and easily overcame the small group who insisted on its being presented. Even Garrick's efforts to quell the mob

[65] Probably Dryden's *Oedipus*.

were futile. Finally the author appeared and asked for permission to withdraw his piece, since it was already condemned in advance. His request was readily granted. But, Archenholz concludes, such disturbances were rare.[66]

One J. H. L. Meyer, whose *Briefe über Russland*[67] seem to have been rather widely read, visited England in the autumn of 1771. His trivial observations were deemed worthy of posthumous publication by Johann Ernst Fabri in his geographical magazine.[68] Meyer describes the superior travelling conditions in England and gives advice on such technical matters as gratuities. He is disgruntled with the troublesome customs officials, against whom Mylius had also complained bitterly,[69] but in general his guide-book reflects the admiration for England common to northern Germans at the time. Agriculture flourishes in Great Britain as in no other country. The inhabitants are industrious and prosperous, straightforward and noble. They are consequently opposed to empty compliments and deceit. Their very frankness and their native integrity account largely for their cool attitude towards foreigners, which has been the subject of much unfavorable comment; for most outsiders, including the Germans, come to England for the sole purpose of enriching themselves, are lacking in the English virtues of honor and uprightness, and introduce evil ways. The British constitution is admirable, but is impaired at present by bribery in high places and by the wretched practice of purchasing seats in Parliament. At the same time there is much unemployment, with hundreds of thousands idle, since the colonies obstinately refuse to buy in the markets of their mother country.

[66] Archenholz' version of this incident is inaccurate. He gives the author's name as O'Kelly, and the year as 1772, whereas it was 1770. Cf. Nicoll, *op. cit.,* pp. 8*ff.*

[67] Göttingen, 1778-1779.

[68] *Bemerkungen auf einer Reise durch Holland, England und Norddeutschland im Jahre 1771 und 1774,* Neues geographisches Magazin, hrsg. von J. E. Fabri. On England, Vol. I, Part 1, pp. 89-102; Vol. II, Part 1, pp. 48-71. Halle, 1785-1786.

[69] *Tagebuch,* August 21, 1753.

This visitor is as vague and superficial in his remarks on the theaters as on other subjects. He has discovered that there are three of them and recklessly estimates that the Haymarket is large enough to accommodate eight thousand spectators; and all are usually so full that not another person could gain admission. The dancers are as good as any to be seen elsewhere, the machinery is superb, and the actors are excellent. As for the audiences, the galleries are only now and then too boisterous in their manifestations of approval or disapproval. They often demand *encores,* even in the presence of the King. A bad actor is not seldom hissed off the stage and is sometimes pelted with lemons. The spectator would do well to take off his hat when the curtain rises and to maintain a discreet silence if he would avoid ejection "in a very unpleasant manner." Likewise he should beware of pickpockets, not only at the doors but within the playhouses. Carelessness in this regard cost poor Meyer himself two pocket-handkerchiefs.

The chief claim on our attention of Heinrich Gottfried von Bretschneider (1739-1810) is his personal acquaintance with Garrick and with Fielding's brother, both of whom he met through his London host, "Daniel Quint, of Windmill Street." Unfortunately, however, he makes no comment on these men. The fragmentary nature of Bretschneider's notes on England is the more regrettable as he is easily the most colorful figure we have encountered since Pöllnitz, and furthermore he included dramatic efforts in his checkered literary career. He bravely begins the account of his journey as "Travels of a german Gentleman through Holland, England and France, for the most part on foot, without money in his pocket." But, apparently exhausted by this linguistic effort, he lapses at once into his native tongue. Presumably Nicolai, with whom this amiable vagabond and typical son of the eighteenth century became acquainted in Berlin in 1773, suggested that he capitalize his recent trip in the form of a book. This appeared in 1817 as *Reise nach London und Paris.* According to Karl Friedrich Linger, Bretschneider's biographer,[70] the writing of the work was not completed until 1801. To the extent that the earlier date, 1773, is tenable, the author may be said to have struck a new note in German literature, for his is in point of time the first of the *Empfindsame Reisen,* of which so many were to be produced, culminating in Heine's *Reisebilder.* Sterne's *Sentimental Journey* appeared in 1768 and within the year was translated into German. No other English book of the century, not excepting *Robinson Crusoe,* made such a deep and lasting impression on the German mind. Something of Sterne's spirit is traceable henceforth in most of the travel literature, yet this represents only the smaller part of his influence. Bretschneider writes Nicolai[71] that he is one of those who travel for their sins (No wonder his travels were so extensive!), and that he will be able to write nothing but a "Sentimental Journey." His determination to avoid the style of Keyssler, whose books of travel were notoriously dull, must have met with the approval of his readers. There is much of interest in the little volume, and still more in the eventful life of its author.

The travel impressions of Friedrich Justinian Freiherr von Günderode, genannt von Kellner, (1747-1785) came out in a gilt-edged, leather-bound volume,[72] easily the handsomest to be found in all the mass of *Reiseliteratur* covered by the pres-

[70] K. F. Linger, *Denkwürdigkeiten aus dem Leben des k. k. Hofrathes H. G. von Bretschneider,* Wien u. Leipzig, 1892; contains a reprint of the *Reisebeschreibung,* which appeared as *Reise nach London und Paris nebst Auszügen aus seinen Briefen an Herrn F. Nicolai,* hrsg. von L. C. F. Göckingk, Berlin und Stettin, 1817. Linger seems to be the only scholar in modern times who has taken an interest in this strange figure.

Bretschneider's parody of *Werther* was reprinted in 1926. It bears the impressive title: *Eine entsetzliche Mordgeschichte von dem jungen Werther, wie sich derselbe den 21. Dezember durch einen Pistolenschuss eigenmächtig ums Leben gebracht. Allen jungen Leuten zur Warnung, und den Alten fast nützlich zu lesen.* Quite likely Nicolai was back of this composition also. The date of publication is given in Meusel's *Das gelehrte Teutschland* as 1774; but Bretschneider wrote Nicolai on January 18, 1776, as if the poem had then been recently completed and would become known at the approaching Frankfurt fair.

[71] October 22, 1774.

[72] *Beschreibung einer Reise aus Teutschland durch einen Theil von Frankreich, England und Holland,* 2 vols. in one, Breslau, 1783.

ent investigation. It is dedicated to the Markgraf von Baden und Hochberg, who had made the same tour. The author, a kinsman of Bettina's unfortunate friend, "die Günderode," was "markgräflicher Badischer Kammerherr zu Carlsruhe" and found time in his career as soldier and courtier to try his hand at dramatic composition.[73] He was a gentle and lovable soul with kind words for everybody and everything. His point of view is consistently that of the South German nobleman of his day, with the usual predilection for things French. He considered it the duty of travellers to record their impressions regularly at the end of each day, and, apparently, to give the public the benefit of their experiences and observations. Günderode set out on his travels in 1774 and seems to have remained abroad until the summer of 1775. He contrived to break in upon Rousseau's seclusion,[74] and he discussed with him the hardships of the voyage from Calais to Dover. He says,[75] "Rousseau told me he had once spent thirteen days on this crossing, having been so driven about by unfavorable winds that he did not arrive until the fourteenth day." It is to be hoped that this statement is no gauge of Günderode's accuracy nor of Rousseau's veracity, for the actual duration of the voyage in question was twelve hours.[76]

With all his personal preference for France, Günderode considered England the most enlightened country in the world.[77] Yet his comparisons of London and Paris are usually to the advantage of the French city. Englishmen are cool and even rude towards strangers, Frenchmen unfailingly polite.[78] Paris is a happier haven for the stranger, for he will make

---

[73] His plays include *Die weibliche Beständigkeit* (1781), *Mariamne* (1781), *Die gelehrte Frau* (1781), and *Das Fest wahrer Freundschaft und Liebe* (1782).

[74] For his account of his visit to Rousseau, see *Beschreibung einer Reise*, Vol. I, pp. 120ff.

[75] *ibid.*, Vol. II, p. 2.

[76] See Collins, J. C., *Voltaire, Montesquieu and Rousseau in England*, London, 1908, p. 201. It is true that on the return trip Rousseau was compelled to await favorable sailing conditions in Dover.

[77] *Beschreibung einer Reise*, Vol. II, p. 213.

[78] *ibid.*, pp. 222, 236.

acquaintances there more readily. In cleanliness, to be sure, the English capital far surpasses the French. The melancholy of the English temperament, so often observed by foreigners, is due in part to the climate.[79] November is known as "hanging month," and suicide is very common in England, though, for that matter, it is on the increase in Germany and France. Evidence of English pride is the capitalization of the pronoun of the first person (!), and an ugly trait in the British character is love of money. This rather trite discourse is relieved by a modern note when the writer predicts that nations will be brought closer together by the increase of travel, and that national characteristics will accordingly become less and less marked.[80]

This German dramatist probably had little sympathy with Lessing's efforts to reform the stage, if he knew anything about them, and still less did he approve of *Sturm und Drang* tendencies:[81] "England is rich in national dramas composed according to the national taste, which is altogether different from the German and French. It is therefore strange that the Germans strive so hard to imitate this taste, which is foreign to us, and which, even if the imitators were successful, would not accord with our national character." He is apparently surprised to find that "Shakespeare's plays are still esteemed in England and many of them frequently performed." Yet Günderode's own dramas have a good measure of *Sturm und Drang* elements traceable to Shakespeare, Rousseau and other sources which their author decried. Despite his theories, he was unable to resist the trend of the times.

As to the relative merits of actors and actresses on the London stage, Günderode opposes Archenholz' views. He saw a number of able actors besides Garrick, but only one female rôle was performed to his complete satisfaction, that of Ophelia. It was doubtless played by Mrs. Smith, whose Ophelia elicited such high praise from Lichtenberg in the

[79] *Beschreibung einer Reise,* Vol. II, pp. 197*ff.*
[80] *ibid.,* p. 241.
[81] *ibid.,* p. 80.

same season. There is in Günderode's opinion no basis of comparison between French and English actors, since the latter must be governed by the taste of their own public and accordingly represent everything more vividly and force-fully:[82] "derer französischen Schauspieler ihr Spiel soll sanft schmelzend, derer Englischen ihres aber hinreissend seyn."[83] But the genius of David Garrick was great enough to vanquish the prejudices even of this confirmed Francophile. He counted himself fortunate to see Garrick as Hamlet, the more so since the celebrated actor's appearances were rare and were soon to cease altogether:[84]

I was all eyes and ears during the performance and was amazed at the extraordinary acting of this man. He was then over sixty years of age,[85] yet he played the part of a young man of twenty with all the verve and sensibility of youth. The melancholy which marked every feature of his face when he made his first appearance, the bold answer which he gives in reply to the King's inquiry into the cause of his sadness, all this won me over to him completely. But later, when the scene with the ghost came, when his soul was stirred to its depths, when he drew his sword and bravely followed the spectre whilst his hair stood on end with horror, I could perceive more plainly than ever that the man had absolute control over his features, and that he was completely absorbed in the impressions of the situation. His scenes with the courtier, with the Queen and with Ophelia were equally masterly. He spoke the famous monolog in the first scene of the third act[86] . . . with the greatest concentration of his whole being. His soul felt at the moment the full import of these words, otherwise he could never have uttered them as he did. I do not hesitate to call Garrick the greatest and most excellent actor of the century.

[82] *ibid.,* p. 81. For Günderode's discussion of the French theater, see Vol. I, pp. 111*ff.*

[83] "The acting of the French is supposed to be gentle and tender, that of the English passionate."

[84] *Beschreibung einer Reise,* Vol. II, pp. 82*ff.*

[85] Garrick was about fifty-eight years old when Günderode saw him.

[86] Here Günderode gives a translation of the monolog.

His sole rival, Günderode adds, is Le Kain, but the French actor never ventures forth from his field of high tragedy, while Garrick is equally at home in tragic and comic rôles.

Like other foreign visitors, Günderode pronounced the settings on the London stage the finest he had ever seen. The producers had begun to devote meticulous care to scenic effects.[87] In this respect of theatrical realism, as in others, England took the lead. The scenes were especially striking "because quite familiar regions, squares, streets and houses of the city" were accurately represented. On one occasion,[88] at a performance of Moore's *Gamester,* when the German spectator's "soul was stirred with all sorts of emotions," he suddenly saw before him "the square, even the very house" in which he lived, and he could scarcely believe his eyes.

Günderode takes issue with Volkmann on the relative decorum of French and English audiences. He suspects, in fact, that Volkmann never saw London, otherwise he would not have made the absurd statement that the theater public was better behaved there than in Paris. On the contrary, it is in public assemblies that the Englishman's lack of restraint is most in evidence.[89] Even the presence of the King and Queen fails to put a quietus on the galleries. Such irreverent demonstrations seem to have been especially offensive to the sensibilities of visiting German noblemen. Baron von Günderode was frequently annoyed by loud conversation and even shouting, and the fusillade of orange-peels from the upper region was the more distressing since substantial portions of them, probably also bits of the fruit, struck him on the head. But he deemed it the part of wisdom to bear such afflictions in silence, and at least he had the satisfaction of observing that his neighbors fared no better than he. To whom could he appeal anyway? There was never a guard in the house. Police supervision would be an intolerable encroachment on the Englishman's personal liberty.

[87] See Nicoll, *op. cit.,* pp. 26*ff.*
[88] *Beschreibung einer Reise,* Vol. II, p. 74.
[89] *ibid.,* pp. 76*ff.*

The Italian opera in London left this visitor cold. He approved of the amphitheater construction of the house, considered the orchestra good and the singing fair, but the ballet poor. "One would think," he says,[90] "that such a strong, muscular people would produce good dancers, but I observed just the contrary. . . . The best of them are foreigners." The audience at the opera, however, was composed largely of decent people (*rechtliche Leute*) and was accordingly more orderly. Günderode visited all the famous places of amusement except Vauxhall, which, to his regret, he was unable to see, as he was not in London during the summer season. He gives an interesting account of his visits to Saddler's Wells, where *rechtliche Leute* were seldom seen, to Ranelagh, where the most interesting sight was the crowds, and to the then new Pantheon, "the handsomest and most magnificent place of the kind anywhere to be found." An especial attraction of both Ranelagh and the Pantheon was the bountiful refreshments which were served to all guests without additional charge.[91]

Although Johann Friedrich Karl Grimm (1737-1821) spent but two months in England (March 12 to May 12, 1774), he succeeded in filling most of two large volumes with his impressions of the country.[92] Grimm was body-physician to the Duke of Saxe-Gotha. His chief interest on his travels was the hospitals and other medical establishments and the scientific museums and collections; but art, literature and theaters also claimed his attention. He had studied medicine under Haller at Göttingen, which of all German universities was naturally the one that bred the strongest English sympathies in its students. Boie, Heyne, Möser, Sturz, Lichtenberg, Binger, Rehberg, Raspe and many other Göttingen professors and students were in the main current of the anglomania which

[90] *ibid.*, p. 88.
[91] *ibid.*, pp. 66*ff*.
[92] *Bemerkungen eines Reisenden durch Deutschland, Frankreich, England und Holland,* 3 vols., Altenburg, 1775. The work appeared anonymously, but is ascribed in Holzmann & Bohatta's *Anonymenlexikon* to Grimm.

swept over Germany in the last third of the eighteenth century. Grimm set out on his journey with a partiality for England which his stay in France en route failed to abate. He may have been somewhat disillusioned in the long run, however, for he discovers that even the British are not perfect,[93] and the motto which he borrowed from Gray for the title-page of his book,

> Life is a jest, and all things show it;
> I thought so once, but now I know it.

suggests that he returned home a sadder and wiser man.

Of the accounts of Channel crossings, in which the *Reise-literatur* abounds, Grimm's is the most harrowing. He suffered intensely for three hours between Calais and Dover and for twenty-five hours between Harwich and Helvoetsluys, and he declared that he would rather engage to run a foot-race for twenty-four hours than to sail for that length of time on the most comfortable ship afloat.[94] We hear from this source the usual praise of English political institutions and of the personal liberty which the island-dwellers enjoy. Both in London and in the country genuine courtesy is more in evidence than in France, though "it is not always expressed in such effusive and ridiculously exaggerated terms."[95] A novel chapter in this book is devoted to the "purchasable women" of Paris and London, whom the author happily likens to bats. The London underworld is a favorite theme with Archenholz also, but Dr. Grimm is more thorough in his treatment of it.

In all the cities on his itinerary Grimm passed many of his evenings in the theater and opera.[96] In Paris he spent at least three evenings a week in the various playhouses, and his conclusion on leaving the city was that "one could see splendid and admirable plays in the capital, although they could not be considered in every respect the most perfect." He leaves us to wonder where "the most perfect" were to be seen; for

[93] *Bemerkungen,* Vol. II, p. 194.
[94] *ibid.,* Vol. III, p. 247.
[95] *ibid.,* p. 193.
[96] *ibid.,* Vol. II, p. 95.

in London he "must confess that the theaters, with all their peculiar merits, fall far short of those in Paris."[97] This judgment is not borne out by his discussion of the performances he attended in the two cities. In London, after Garrick, it is King, Jefferson, Aiken and Moody, Mrs. Hopkins, Mrs. Smith and Mrs. Abington who please him most. While the actors at Covent Garden were very good, he was always drawn towards Drury Lane, whether through "prejudice in favor of the owner, or for some other reason" he knew not. He apparently saw Garrick only in *The provok'd Wife* and *Hamlet*. Of the former performance he says nothing. As for Garrick's Hamlet, the scene with the ghost drew from him "a cold death-sweat." Garrick is Proteus himself:[98]

> He had a rather round face and lively eyes when I saw him, for I believe one never sees him in his true form. Whether it be nature or art (the former, I firmly believe), he has the slightest muscle of his body and especially of his face under such control that he can represent all the emotions of the soul so that others may see them plainly. A great quality of the man is that he speaks so distinctly that one can understand his voice, which naturally carries well, in every corner of the house. His mere appearance and his figure instantly reveal even to the most untrained eye what he is.

Grimm was also impressed by the staging of the plays he saw in London:[99]

> Nothing is lacking in the way of scenery. The decorations are lavish, and the setting is changed whenever a new scene demands. The effects are dazzling. The costumes are genuine, of gold, silver and silk.

The oratorios, usually by Händel, which were to be heard twice a week during Lent, were not remarkable for the voices,[100] nor were the operas superior to those of other cities

[97] *Bemerkungen*, Vol. III, p. 219.
[98] *ibid.*, p. 218.
[99] *ibid.*, p. 215.
[100] *ibid.*, Vol. II, p. 360.

except in the magnificence of the costumes.[101] Some of the
opera singers were excellent, but Grimm could take no pleasure in the warbling of the *castrati,* "whose voices sound quite
hoarse and strike the ear like the crowing of a cock." Of them
all, Signor Millico, the idol of Miss Burney's heroine,
Evelina, was to Grimm the most objectionable, both as singer
and actor. The audiences in theater and opera seemed orderly
enough, far more so than in Paris :[102]

> The spectators refrain from applause and laughter until
> the end of the speech or song, disturbing neither the lis-
> tener in his attention nor the actor in the performance
> of his rôle. If one were not otherwise aware of being
> amongst a serious people on this island, one would be
> convinced of the fact at the plays. The unbearable jubila-
> tion and shouting of the French over every little trifle,
> for instance when a singer does a trill or sustains a note
> unusually long, or a dancer leaps up in the air, is never
> heard here, except now and then when an irrepressible
> youth raises his voice.

Most of the German visitors who recorded their impressions of England after Voltaire published his *Lettres philosophiques* (1734) repeated with some variations what the
Frenchman had written concerning the honor paid to the
great men and women of the nation both in their lifetime and
after their death. Grimm, too, commends this English custom
and rejoices in the monuments in Westminster Abbey to
great poets, actors, composers and scholars.[103] Only recently
a monument had been erected to Mrs. Pritchard beside that
of Shakespeare, and Garrick's fame and fortune were sufficient to assure him a memorial among those of kings, "for
in this country the art of actors, without respect of person
and regardless of moral conduct, is an honored art, far more
so than in Germany and France."

An especially interesting book of travel, yet one that is
apparently forgotten, is that of Franz Paula Graf von Hartig

[101] *Bemerkungen,* Vol. III, pp. 208*ff.*
[102] *ibid.,* pp. 216*ff.*
[103] *ibid.,* Vol. II, p. 460.

(1758-1797). It is composed of letters to a friend written on a journey through France, England and Italy in the years 1775-1776. The first letter gives an account of the coronation of Louis XVI at Rheims, and the last before those from Italy tells of a visit to Voltaire at Geneva. Hartig was a member of a distinguished Austrian family and held important positions in the diplomatic service of his country. He was a favorite of Maria Theresa and of Joseph II, and it was in compliance with the Emperor's wishes, it is said, that the young count sought on his travels to gain insight into European politics. He was a man of marked ability. His *Mélanges de Vers et de Prose* (1788) won the approval of the French Academy. As a son of the higher German nobility, his education had been thoroughly French. Had he grown up in the shadow of the court of Versailles, in fact, he could not well have been more imbued with French culture. Considered from this angle, his letters throw an interesting light on the German intellectual life of the day, for they show that even in court circles there was an increasing tendency to appraise importations from France more critically and to recognize merit and at least some promise of creative genius in the German mind. The well known views of Frederick the Great advanced in his essay *Sur la Littérature allemande* (1780) must have fallen on deaf ears in many quarters. Hartig may be allowed to speak at some length for himself. He writes from Paris:[104]

> I have now been living for three months in a city which we Germans look upon with admiration and high esteem, a city of which we accept the fashions as laws, the vices as lessons in decency, and the language as that knowledge which is essential to distinguish man from animal.

He for one will not be ashamed of his mother-tongue when

---

[104] *Lettres sur la France, l'Angleterre et l'Italie,* Genève, 1785; German trans., *Interessante Briefe über Frankreich, England und Italien,* Eisenach, 1786, p. 21. (References are to the German ed., which is rare; copy found in the Universitätsbibliothek, Marburg.)

he returns home. He also thinks that the French stage is overrated:[105]

> French plays, with which all Europe is so smitten, also claim the leisure hours of every tourist. The prestige of the French stage, and their own prejudices cause the spectators to see only the perfections and to overlook the flaws. It would be an offense against good taste if a young German on his return from Paris could find another play bearable after having seen a performance of Le Kain or of Mlle. Raucourt.

He continues in this vein:[106]

> The French theater affords me in general the greatest pleasure without arousing my enthusiasm, and I am convinced that we shall soon reach in Germany that degree of perfection to which the French stage has with some justification laid claim.

However, greater discrimination must control the selection of the German repertoire:

> The reliance of our authors on the great indulgence of the public accounts for the careless composition of their dramatic pieces. Our German stage is consequently flooded with very mediocre comedies and equally poor tragedies. . . . Such excessive indulgence appears to me the more inexcusable, since the quantity of excellent German plays with which so many geniuses have enriched our stage justifies a firm stand against mediocre products. . . . Yet we now debase our stage with tragedies which are simply dull novels in the form of poor dialogue, or with comedies which abound in the most vulgar conversations composed in the taste of the rabble.

Whatever the merits of their offerings, the Paris theaters, with the exception of the Opera House, were unworthy of the city; "in fact, our German theaters surpass them in architectural design and in magnificence."

Despite his critical attitude the young count was loath to leave the French with their "charming frivolity." Yet he

[105] *Lettres*, p. 22.
[106] *ibid.*, pp. 36*ff*.

took comfort in the thought that he was to return to France on his way to Italy, and meanwhile was to spend some time among the "proud and free Britons." While at Calais, where he was compelled to wait a full fortnight for favorable weather, he saw some German troops who had been shipwrecked on their way to America and was impressed by the kind treatment which the unfortunate men, though belonging to a hostile nation, received at the hands of the French. He found distraction during his wait in the society of Lord and Lady Spencer and Admiral H.[107] and especially the latter's charming daughter Marianne, "ein göttliches Mädchen" endowed with "intelligence, beauty, charm, talents, everything." In fact, young Hartig was confronted with the danger of "losing his freedom among a free people." His knowledge of the English language stood him in good stead, for the Admiral spoke no other tongue, although Miss Marianne had a fluent command of both French and Italian. After having seen more representatives of the species, his admiration for English women was only increased. They were exceedingly beautiful, far more so than the French, and had no need of art to enhance their native charms. Hartig found travel in England a pleasure that only a possible encounter with highwaymen might spoil,[108] "beautiful roads, excellent horses, postillions who drive admirably and are not so impudent as many French postillions, abundant hospitality in the inns, even if one is stopping only for a rest." Coming from an Austria in which liberalism was beginning to dawn under the influence of Joseph II, he was full of admiration for English liberty and for the constitution by which it was guaranteed. Soon after his arrival he was presented at court, where he witnessed the cool reception given to General Gage, who had just returned from America. He found many partisans of the American cause in London,[109] "many true patriots

[107] Presumably Admiral Howe, son of the second Viscount Howe and Maria Sophia von Kielmannsegge. He had a daughter, Maria Juliana, probably the Marianne in question.
[108] *Lettres,* p. 90.
[109] *ibid.,* p. 99.

who look upon the American war as the grave of their freedom and of English greatness, who maintain openly that the
Americans would never have taken up arms against their
mother country if they had not been refused the privileges
of the British constitution and British law."

Again Hartig congratulated himself on his command of
the English language, for it enabled him to understand what
he heard in the theaters. His visit fell in the last year of
Garrick's stage career, and the great actor was then appearing
twice a week. Hartig refrains from a criticism of his acting, on
the ground that Garrick's fame was already sufficiently well
known. He became personally acquainted with him and admired him for his intellect and knowledge.[110] In his criticism
of English plays the young Austrian is true to his French
schooling. Many English comedies are funny, he observes,
many lachrymose. Though a number of them are excellent, he
still prefers the French theater, "in which delicacy is observed
both in the choice of ideas and in the character of the personages." The Englishman, on the other hand, attempts to re-
produce nature too closely, frequently causing it to appear in
a coarse and repellent form. The monarch and the hero
should speak on the stage in all situations according to the
dignity of their position. The idea of grandeur must be maintained in order to win the spectator's admiration. Who can
admire the hero when he talks like a peasant? There may be
in actual life moments when the hero's language is similar
to the peasant's, but these lapses should not be represented on
the stage. Realism is for the historian, not for the dramatist.
"The painting of a Raphael must not be disfigured by the
brush of a Callot." Even Shakespeare's admirable tragedies
are often marred by such touches, but there are always sub-
lime passages, such as Hamlet's monolog, to compensate for
the occasional crudities. And again the poor *Stürmer und
Dränger* are taken to task:

> Some German writers have attempted to imitate Shake-
> speare in their tragedies, for that is the taste of the day.

[110] *Lettres*, pp. 116*ff*., on English theaters.

They have shown great skill in causing dead bodies to fall on the stage. But to copy those delicate strokes of wit and reason, those lively expressions of the soul, is to be sure more difficult than the slaughter of a half dozen characters.

Hartig found *opera seria* in London on a high plane. Upon hearing *Xerxes* sung in English he concluded that that language was quite as singable as French, despite the prevalent impression to the contrary. But the English spoiled artists by rewarding their talents so extravagantly. At a private recital the young courtier actually saw a princess of the blood on her knees before the celebrated prima donna Gabrielli, vainly imploring her to sing. Hartig's real enthusiasm, however, was reserved for the operettas of the Théâtre Italien in Paris. As for French grand opera, though he realized that it was little short of blasphemy to say so, it was distasteful to him and sometimes had an almost irresistible soporific effect upon him.[111]

While Johann Georg Büsch (1728-1800) has nothing to say of theatrical performances in London, his account of his travels in England is worthy of notice here as something of an anomaly in its category.[112] Although the author was educated at Göttingen, that seat of Anglophiles, he expresses a minimum of admiration for England and the English. It is only in industry and commerce, his particular field, that he recognizes leadership in the British nation. He states explicitly that he finds the Dutch more congenial than any other people.[113] Both the content and the style of his book belie the prestige of its author, for he was the founder of a famous *Handelsakademie* in Hamburg and made a valuable contribution to the infant science of *Nationalökonomie* in his *Abhandlung von dem Geldumlauf,* for which he did the main research in England. A book of travel is to a great extent autobiographical. Büsch reveals himself as provincial,

[111] *Lettres,* pp. 38f.
[112] *Bemerkungen auf einer Reise durch einen Theil der Vereinigten Niederlande und Englands,* Hamburg, 1786.
[113] *ibid.,* p. 31.

narrow-minded and conceited; and as a traveller, a Smollett
rather than a Sterne. When Uffenbach's diary was published
in 1753, Büsch, so he says, conceived the idea of writing on
the travels of a *reisende Handwerksbursche* in Uffenbach's style, and that is on the whole what he inadvertently
did some thirty years later. He visited England in 1777,[114]
dividing a summer vacation of ten weeks between that country and Holland, but did not write of his travel impressions
until after the appearance of Moritz' account of his trip to
England in 1782. He agreed with Archenholz and others in
the opinion that Professor Moritz should have known better
than to undertake a tour of England on foot.[115] He had read
Archenholz and Wendeborn, and took pleasure in putting
them right on certain points.[116] The chief merit of this writer
is his brevity. He makes the sensible observation that a traveller in describing an already well known country should have
an eye rather to what he omits than to what he includes.

Büsch seems to be the first of our German tourists to include excessive materialism among the national traits of the
British. They are the only people, so far as he knows,[117] who
estimate a man's worth in terms of his income. It would be
interesting to know at what time in the nineteenth century
this distinction was transferred in the popular German mind
from the Britisher to the American.

If it made no particular impression on him otherwise, the
theater did at least afford Büsch evidence of the peculiar
English spirit of freedom and independence:[118]

> I went to the theater in Richmond. The house was well
> filled, especially the gallery. Suddenly a cry was raised
> by a number of voices at the same moment: "Throw
> her down! Throw her down!" I thought it applied to an
> actress who was just then giving a very mediocre per-

[114] Büsch says he left Hamburg on July 19, but does not mention the
year. It is fixed, however, by the statement (p. 109) that the news of
Burgoyne's capturing Ticonderoga arrived while he was in London.
[115] *Bemerkungen*, p. 97.
[116] *ibid.*, pp. 122, 209.
[117] *ibid.*, p. 173.
[118] *ibid.*, p. 118.

formance. The actors paused, and I was prepared for the worst. Then something really was thrown down from the gallery, I know not what. . . . Similar disturbances occurred in those quarters several more times, and each time the actors, being quite accustomed to such interruptions, very calmly paused.

If Pöllnitz, Bretschneider and others we have followed on their travels bear the unmistakable stamp of the eighteenth century, Karl Friedrich Bahrdt (1741-1792) is not less representative of that age of Freemasons, Rosicrucians, Socinians, Illuminati, Cagliostros, and Chevaliers d'Éon. A "theological adventurer," he began his remarkable career as an orthodox clergyman, a favorite of the steadfast Pastor Goeze, who dared to match swords with Lessing. But he soon abandoned the orthodox cause to run the whole gamut of existing theological schools and finally to found one of his own. His aim was the abolition of all positive religions and the establishment of a purely naturalistic religion based on universal reason. His chief theological work was his *Neueste Offenbarungen Gottes,* which called forth a humorous *Prolog* from Goethe.[119] By Kotzebue he was dubbed "Bahrdt mit der eisernen Stirn." The purpose of his trip to England in 1777-1778 was to enlist disciples for his *Institut* at Oppenheim, which was one of his schemes for reforming the world and at the same time improving his own lot in it. Reinhold Forster and his eldest son, George, befriended him and assisted him in presenting his cause to an indifferent English public. He also became acquainted with Erich Raspe, "the former professor in Kassel,"[120] who is known as the

[119] *Neueste Offenbarungen Gottes in Briefen und Erzählungen,* Giessen, 1774; for Goethe's *Prolog,* see *Werke,* Weimar ed., Vol. XVI, pp. 107 *ff.*

[120] Bahrdt, *Geschichte seines Lebens, von ihm selbst geschrieben,* Part 1, Frankfurt a. M., 1790; Parts 2-4, Berlin, 1791; *Reise nach London,* Part 3, pp. 289-381; see p. 329. Extracts from *Geschichte seines Lebens* and a sketch of Bahrdt's life appear in *Deutsche Literatur, Reihe Deutsche Selbstzeugnisse,* Vol. VIII, Leipzig, 1934.

Dr. Raspe is frequently mentioned by German visitors to London. He eked out a living as a hack-writer and translator and doubtless contributed more to the exchange of literary wares between England and

author or compiler of the English original of the Baron
Münchhausen stories, which Bürger later converted into a
German classic. The only real champion Bahrdt won for his
cause in London was the kind-hearted Dr. Wendeborn, who
in this instance subsequently had occasion to regret his
benevolence. Despite such support, the reformer met with but
little success and was in the most straitened circumstances
during his stay in England.

Undaunted by the failure of his plans, Bahrdt was delighted with what he saw of English life and English people,
and felt strongly tempted to settle permanently in London.[121]
With his heterodox religious views he might have done better
to choose Pennsylvania. He considered the English "the
most perfect nation" with which he was acquainted,[122] but by
nation he meant the middle classes, "for the nobility in
England is indeed corrupt. It is under the sway of French
luxury, French intrigue and French vices." The real national
character of the Englishman is founded upon freedom and
virtue. "The true Englishman is noble and loyal and absolutely incapable of a mean act or a violation of the rules of
fair dealing."[123] But there was more evidence of poverty and
misery in London than this war-time visitor had ever seen
elsewhere.

Bahrdt was frank enough to say that he did not understand
the English language, this being the first time that we hear
such a confession. But in spite of his linguistic handicap he
went to Covent Garden Theatre, so he claims, where he saw
The Skol of Skandals. As *The School for Scandal* was first

Germany than will ever be known. Most works such as his appeared
anonymously at that time, and in his case anonymity may have been
especially desirable, for his expatriation was not voluntary. New and valuable material on Raspe appears in R. Hallo's *Rudolf Erich Raspe, ein
Wegbereiter von deutscher Art und Kunst,* Göttinger Forschungen, Vol. V,
Stuttgart und Berlin, 1934. Raspe's contribution to the *Sturm und Drang*
movement was considerable. On his sponsorship of the "Gothic" period
of German culture, and of Ossian and the *Volkslied,* see Hallo, especially
Part 2, Chaps. I and II.

[121] *Geschichte seines Lebens,* p. 353.
[122] *ibid.,* p. 357.
[123] *ibid.,* p. 358.

produced at Drury Lane on May 8, 1777, Bahrdt appears to
have made a slip. Wherever it was and whatever he saw, he
considered "the actors far more perfect than in Germany"
and "the declamation and pantomime more masterly" than
on any German stage.[124]

The picture of England by Johann Reinhold Forster
(1729-1798)[125] is but little more favorable than the one by
Büsch. In Forster's case, however, there is an explanation. He
had accompanied Cook on his second world tour, 1772-1775,
and felt, not without some justification, that the recognition
and reward due him for the scientific work he had done on
the expedition had been withheld. As a result his whole out-
look on England and on the world at large was darkened.

The name of Reinhold Forster was better known in England than that of any other of the German visitors. He was
a native of Schleswig and a descendant of Scotch emigrants
who had settled in East Prussia in the seventeenth century. In
1766 he removed with his family to London, where he made
his home until 1783, when he accepted a call to Halle. His
studies in natural history yielded valuable results, and he was
a pioneer in the field of comparative geography. Even without the strong personal bias reflected therein, however, his
book on England would be of little interest now, and it
apparently gained little recognition in its day. Its origin was
altogether inauspicious. The motive behind it, aside from
purposes of retaliation, was economic necessity. George Forster, with more critical insight than filial piety, pronounced
it a "miserable pasquil,"[126] and he felt that some of the
animosity it had aroused had been transferred from father
to son, hampering the latter in his career in England.

[124] *ibid.*, p. 369. Bahrdt was doubtless at Drury Lane, in spite of what
he says. No wonder he praised the actors. It was a brilliant cast: King
as Sir Peter, Mrs. Abington as Lady Teazle, Smith as Charles Surface,
Palmer as Joseph Surface, Miss Sherry as Lady Sneerwell, and Mrs. Pope
as Mrs. Candour. "The minor parts were equally well filled." See Sichel,
W., *Sheridan*, 2 vols., London, 1909, Vol. I, pp. 578ff.

[125] *Tableau d'Angleterre pour l'Année 1780 continué par l'Éditeur
jusqu'à l'Année 1783*, place of publication not named, 1783.

[126] *Briefe und Tagebücher*, Halle, 1893, p. 117.

We learn from Reinhold Forster that the fine arts are protected and encouraged in England, but more as the gratification of a whim or with the desire for display than from personal taste. The Englishman is "swept off his feet by the torrent of fashion, but lacks critical standards of art."[127] The dramatists worth mentioning are Dryden, Addison, Goldsmith and Armstrong. Cumberland is referred to, but not as a dramatist. The theater has lost Garrick, "the foremost actor of his times, even eclipsing Le Kain," but Henderson gives promise of filling the vacant place. King, Palmer, Yates and Moody are but second-rate actors. Mrs. Yates, Mrs. Crawford and Miss Younge are excellent actresses, especially in tragedy, and Mrs. Abington continues to hold her own. As for English music, it is altogether in the hands of foreigners, the best among them being Germans. Bach, Abel, Fischer, Cramer and many others reflect credit upon their native country.[128] Accomplished singers and dancers are likewise invariably imported from the Continent.

Like Forster, Johann Christian Fabricius (1743-1808) was a native of Schleswig. His family removed to Copenhagen, where he attended the university, having prepared himself at the Altona *Gymnasium*. He subsequently entered the University of Upsala, where he was the student and intimate friend of Linné.[129] In the course of his distinguished career as a scientist Fabricius was for many years "Professor der Naturgeschichte, Oekonomie und Cameralwissenschaft" at Kiel. With the versatility of his times, he also lectured on botany, entomology, mineralogy and other subjects. As a member of the "Royal Societies of Denmark, Norway, Berlin, London and Leipzig," he kept in touch with scholars everywhere. He was an intimate friend of Sir Joseph Banks and an admirer of the unlovable Professor Büsch. He paid

---

[127] *Tableau d'Angleterre,* p. 170.

[128] *ibid.,* pp. 171ff.

[129] According to the article on Fabricius in the *A.D.B.*, he entered the university at Copenhagen in 1762. He himself says (Article on Linné, *Deutsches Museum,* May-July, 1780) that he began in that year his studies under, and close association with, Linné, which continued for two years.

frequent visits to England, the one of which he wrote having extended through the summer of 1782. His book is a series of letters, the literary form which seems most likely to be produced when a writer follows the line of least resistance, and which the example of Richardson and Rousseau fixed upon the literature of travel even more tenaciously than upon the novel.

It is safe to say that it was the scientists, of all foreigners, who were most richly rewarded by their visits to England, both on account of English preeminence in the sciences and because of the inherently greater facility in the international exchange of ideas in the scientific realm than in other branches of culture. Fabricius owed much to his English contacts and repaid his debt by swelling the volume of praise for Britain. Though he touches on the darker side of English life, such as highway robbery, the empressment of sailors, and poverty and vice in London, he brings out many more lights than shadows. He maintains that no foreigner who stays long enough in England to adapt himself to the peculiarities in customs and manners, can fail to enjoy the life there, and these very peculiarities will eventually prove to be the chief source of satisfaction. He revels, like Lichtenberg, in the rich variety and busy stir of London life, and is delighted with the scenic beauty of the country, with the unfailing hospitality of the people, and the absolute freedom of speech and action. He deplores, on the other hand, the intellectual isolation of the British. They know little of foreign literature and less of foreign scholarship. "Sir Joseph Banks is perhaps the only man who obtains everything that pertains to his field."[130] The *Göttinger Anzeiger*, the *Allgemeine Deutsche Bibliothek* and all the latest scientific publications of Germany are to be found in his library. "He himself, however, neither reads nor understands them, but provides them for scholars and foreigners who wish to use his library." This criticism, frequently voiced in some form or

[130] *Briefe aus London vermischten Inhalts*, Dessau u. Leipzig, 1784; see pp. 337-8.

other by foreign visitors, was undoubtedly just. In this case
it is certainly colored by no personal prejudice. Fabricius
candidly acknowledges English supremacy in the sciences.[131]

Since Fabricius gives an interesting account of the decline
of the London stage after Garrick's retirement, he is quoted
at length.[132] He was an ardent lover of the theater, and with
his usual candor confesses his partiality to the English stage,
the first with which he became well acquainted and the one,
accordingly, that formed his taste:

> The force, the passion of speech and action in London
> theatrical performances spoiled my taste for the various
> others that I have come to know. If we are accustomed
> to drinking brandy, wine seems like water, and I confess,
> accordingly, that I have found the French theater even
> in Paris extremely dull. But the English theater is by no
> means what it was during my first visit to London, in
> 1767-1768. At that time I had the good fortune to see
> several actors and actresses, any one of whom could have
> assured the success of the theater. Garrick, Foote, King,
> Powell, Weston, Barry, Smith, Shuter, Mrs. Pritchard,
> Yates, Dancer, Clive, Abington, Arne, made the English
> stage at that time the most brilliant in Europe. But most
> of them are long since dead, and of those surviving some
> [sic] have grown older and others are dispersed.

This *laudator temporis acti* adds that a few of these celebrities are still to be seen in London in the winter season, but
now (in August) are either taking vacations or filling pro-
fessional engagements in Dublin. Owing to difficulties with
the management, Mrs. Crawford, formerly Mrs. Dancer, has
not appeared in London for several years, but is permanently attached to the Dublin theater. Among the younger
actors Henderson and Miss Younge have won deserved
recognition, but have by no means reached the height of a
Garrick or Powell, or of a Yates or Crawford. Since Foote's
death the Haymarket has also declined. This great comedian,

---

[131] *Briefe*, Introduction.
[132] *ibid.*, pp. 166*ff.*, for the discussion of the English stage.

whom Fabricius apparently knew personally, was irreplace-
able :

> His inexhaustible, trenchant humor and his peculiar gift
> of caricature are inimitable. No actor has ever equalled
> him, whether he was representing the old procuress
> known all over the city or the Methodist enthusiast
> Whitefield or any other such (!) character. It was cari-
> cature to be sure, but it was so perfectly true to life that
> he never failed to elicit our laughter and hearty applause.
> I still have pleasant memories of a piece that was first
> produced in 1768, called *The Devil upon two Sticks*. It
> dealt with a remarkable, quibbling controversy among
> some physicians, and the whole piece was so humorous
> and the acting withal so comical that, so the story went
> at the time, an apothecary actually died of laughter in
> the theater. A fact it is at any rate that the piece was
> performed over forty times during the season, and the
> last time, when the doors were to be closed, enough
> people were turned away to fill two more houses.

But Foote is no more, and his plays, like all works treating
of personages and incidents of transitory interest, have lost
their appeal. His successor, Colman, is an able playwright,
but not an actor. Apparently aware of his company's limita-
tions, he generally produces farces, pantomimes and the like,
and although they are tastefully and admirably executed, one
or two such entertainments are enough. Mrs. Abington is as
remarkable as ever, but the slightest annoyance is sufficient
to give her a headache, whereupon she excuses herself for the
evening, even though it be the very moment for the curtain
to rise.

Fabricius mentions disparagingly *"The fatal Curiosity* by
old Lillo, the author of *Barnwell."* He saw it in Colman's
adaptation, which had its première during his stay in London. "It is a mediocre play," he writes, "and a still more
mediocre performance caused it to appear in a most disagreeable light. . . . It might, without any loss to the English theater, have remained in the oblivion into which it
had fallen."—Yet "old Lillo," after Shakespeare, is the

English dramatist to whom German literature owes most!

It was Fabricius' custom to pay a visit to Saddler's Wells on each of his trips to London.[133] Quite to the taste of the common man, by whom it was principally patronized, this place of amusement offered more for the money than any other. The best seats cost only three shillings, and for that modest outlay one could enjoy an operetta, a ballet, a pantomime, a variety of acrobatic performances, and a quarter bottle of wine. As for Ranelagh and Vauxhall, they surpassed all such entertainments in other countries.[134] All imitations of them on the Continent appeared small and mean in comparison, lacking the extraordinary splendor of their London models. Ranelagh was especially magnificent, but to enjoy it fully one must have a wide acquaintance in the higher social circles. Vauxhall was more democratic. There Fabricius had spent many happy evenings in his youth.

The Seven Years' War marks an almost abrupt change in the German attitude towards England, as the writings of our *Englandfahrer* plainly show. Practically all of them now and for some time to come are subject in varying degrees to anglomania. At first it is largely the admiration of the newly enlightened German mind for the great seat of enlightenment, but gradually an element of *Sturm und Drang* fervor creeps into the German appraisal of things English, and England comes to be regarded as the country where nature and freedom reign supreme and man may realize in the fullest measure his manifest destiny. Typical representatives of the enlightened school of thought are Möser, Sturz and Lichtenberg, but all other German visitors as well, save two, in the period 1763-1780 voice their admiration for English institutions and English culture. The writings of the two dissenters, Büsch and Reinhold Forster, were not of sufficient weight to affect materially the general estimate of England or to influence appreciably German opinion. In the case of Forster, this unfavorable attitude is fully explained by

[133] *Briefe,* pp. 173*ff.*
[134] *ibid.,* pp. 261*ff.*

his personal grievances against certain individual Englishmen.

In these years we find for the first time a group of Germans to whom a broad cultural background and a certain degree of critical taste and insight are common. Accustomed to seeing good plays well performed in Hamburg or some other German city, they were better equipped than their predecessors to evaluate the offerings of the London stage, and with the perspective they thus possessed, they were able to reach a certain degree of objectivity in their criticisms. Not only Lichtenberg, but Sturz, Fabricius and others were capable of forming opinions that may be accepted as reliable.

Justus Möser is the first of the travellers to express his scorn for the French dramatic tradition and to suggest specifically that German dramatists might learn valuable lessons from the English. Later on Sturz and Lichtenberg, following Lessing's lead, loudly decry French classicism and recommend English models to German playwrights. Here Günderode is the chief representative of the opposition. He still classes Germany with France in dramatic taste. In this he has the support of Hartig, who, while recognizing advancement in German drama, still looks to France instead of England for standards of perfection. Both, however, reflect the particular point of view of the courtier and appear moreover to be less positive in their French leanings than an earlier generation of German noblemen.

The first German to present a thoughtful criticism of English acting is Helferich Peter Sturz. Others before him had praised performances they had witnessed in London, but he was able to analyze his impressions and give valid reasons for his judgments. The dominant figure of the English stage at this time was, of course, David Garrick. Möser failed to see him, and this misfortune doubtless accounts to some extent for his lack of enthusiasm. To him the English performance of tragedy seemed violent and grotesque, as it had to Muralt and Mylius. He alone of this group expressed a preference for comedy to tragedy on the English stage. Without exception all attested to the beauty, magnificence and effectiveness of the stage settings and scenery, frequently declaring that London theaters surpassed in this respect those of all other countries. There is some difference of opinion as to the behavior of the spectators. Archenholz defends the English theater audience, though he takes account of the usual pandemonium in the gallery before the curtain rises; but Günderode and even Grimm, who ordinarily delights in fulminating against the French, declare that much better order is observed in the theaters of Paris. The decline of the London stage with the passing of Garrick is stressed by Fabricius. Even Mrs. Siddons was scarcely able to offset this loss. The undeniable deterioration of the English theater which begins about this period is reflected in the views of German critics during the rest of the century.

CHAPTER III

PEAK OF ANGLOMANIA

THE best known book on England written by a German
in the eighteenth century is the *Travels*[1] of Karl Philipp
Moritz (1757-1793), 1782. This little volume has gone
through many editions. An English translation appeared in
1795 and was reprinted several times within the next few
years. In 1903 a scholarly German edition was published,[2]
and in 1924 the original English version was reprinted with
an interesting introduction and notes by P. E. Matheson.[3]
The books of Fabricius and Moritz, dating from the same
year, are in striking contrast, and afford excellent docu-
mentation of the two distinct currents of anglomania in Germany, rationalist and *Sturm und Drang.* Fabricius falls in
line with such men as Alberti, Lichtenberg and Sturz, who
admired the English for their enlightenment and intellectual
independence, while Moritz, a somewhat belated *Stürmer und
Dränger,* was possessed of vague enthusiasm for the naïveté,
spontaneity, colorfulness, individualism and personal liberty
of English life. Fabricius felt at home in an orderly world
governed by reason, while Moritz thrilled to opportunities
of self-expression. These points of view were not mutually
exclusive, but were sufficiently clear-cut to mark a division
into two schools of thought. The rationalist viewed the English scene from Voltaire's angle of vision, the *Stürmer und
Dränger* as Rousseau might have, had he gone to England
in his youth. Fabricius is in some respects an intellectual
descendant of Lessing, while Moritz belongs to the spiritual
progeny of Hamann, whose own awakening to the obscure

[1] *Reisen eines Deutschen in England im Jahre 1782,* Berlin, 1783.
[2] Ed. by Otto zur Linde, in *Deutsche Literaturdenkmale des 18. Jahrhunderts,* no. 126.
[3] Oxford University Press.

forces of nature and the subconscious promptings of the soul was effected at least in part by his residence in England.[4]

As a Hanoverian, Moritz had ready access to the storehouses of English culture. We read in his autobiographical novel, *Anton Reiser,* one of the most important revelations of the *Sturm und Drang* soul, that the first friend of his comparatively friendless childhood was an English gentleman. At the age of ten he began to acquire the English language by speaking it with this benefactor, and henceforth he is diligent in the study of both the language and the literature of the country to which he felt bound by ties of spiritual affinity. In the opening paragraph of his book on England he declares that it had been his most cherished wish for years to visit that country. The absorbing passion of his youth was Shakespeare and the stage. That he knew and loved Sterne, the reader of his English *Travels* will not need to be told. Even more than Bahrdt, or any other German imitator of Sterne up to his time, he writes a "sentimental journey." With all his enthusiasm for England and English literature, however, Moritz is less lavish in his praise of the country than the majority of German visitors. He had several unpleasant experiences which he brought upon himself by undertaking a foot-tour. He must have appeared almost as conspicuous as would a man tramping through the English countryside at the present time in the garb of a Tyrolean mountaineer. Many were the voices raised in protest on both sides of the Channel against such a method of locomotion in England. Apparently Moritz was one of the few who were unaware that it was not the thing to do. He had evidently overestimated the operations of individual liberty in the land of his dreams. Archenholz, Büsch, Lehzen, were amazed at his ignorance.

On reading Moritz' accounts of the theatrical performances[5] he witnessed, we cannot fail to regret that his visit coincided with the decline of the stage and also that he

---

[4] April 1757-July 1758.
[5] For Moritz' discussion of theaters, see *Reisen,* Linde's ed., pp. 41ff.

was in London only in the summer season, his whole journey
having extended from the end of May to the middle of July.
As it was, he considered but few of the actors at all remarkable. He evidently saw only three plays, Foote's *Nabob*,
O'Keefe's *The agreeable Surprise*, and Colman's *The English Merchant.*[6] Owing to its local and personal nature, much
of the *Nabob* was lost on him. Yet he was pleased with Palmer in the title-rôle and found the scenes "with the Quakers
and with the Society of Natural Research" exceedingly amusing.[7] But the high spot was the scene between the Nabob and
his former friend and schoolmate, a rôle which was played
by Edwin. The old friend is all expansive good-nature, but he
is relentlessly snubbed by the purse-proud parvenu.

As a schoolmaster with a sense of humor, Moritz is delighted with *The agreeable Surprise,* a comic opera in which
the pedantic pedagog is held up to ridicule. The pedant,
Moritz observes, is just as familiar a figure in England as
elsewhere and just as properly the target of satire on the
London stage as on any other. Edwin was irresistible in the
rôle of the schoolmaster. A certain good-natured expression
always discernible in this actor's face, no matter what part
he played, won the spectator over to him and rendered the
character he represented doubly interesting. The audience
was so pleased with Edwin's performance in this instance
that he was compelled to sing himself hoarse in response
to the demand of the gallery for *encores,* and besides had to
express his thanks for the applause repeatedly by profound
bows. Mrs. Webb's rotundity and her whole appearance fitted
her admirably for the part of the cheese-monger, so that she
represented the common woman with a realism new to this
veteran theater-goer. So charmed was Moritz with O'Keefe's
rather feeble play that he wished to translate it into German,
but discovered that it had not yet appeared in print.

Of *The English Merchant* Moritz had seen a better presentation in Hamburg. Fleck, in his opinion, had put more

[6] Based on Voltaire's *Le Café, ou l'Écossaise.*
[7] *recte*, the Christian Club and the Antiquarian Society.

"Interesse, Wahrheit und Biederkeit" into the rôle of Freeport, the merchant, than did Aiken. He and other members of the cast, including Palmer as the journalist Spatter, had too much of the English gentleman about them for the parts in which they were cast. The rôle of Amalia was taken by an actress who was making her first appearance at the Haymarket and seemed to be too timid to speak audibly. But when a voice from the upper gallery shouted "Speak louder, O speak louder!", she managed to make herself heard.

This genial visitor did not escape the fate common to foreigners in English playhouses. Oranges no longer fresh descended in abundance in his neighborhood, one or more striking his head, which fortunately was protected at the moment by his hat. The poor victim dared not look around lest he receive a broadside in the face. Oranges were cheap in London at that time, he observed.

Vauxhall and Ranelagh appealed to Moritz for the opportunities they afforded of watching the crowds and studying human nature. Vauxhall was so strangely similar to its Berlin namesake that an evening there caused this eighteenth-century Odysseus pangs of homesickness. Thus with all his *Wanderlust,* which later took him to Italy, he was easily susceptible to *Heimweh* and was accordingly a typical German. As for Ranelagh, he had often heard of the place, but had no idea what went on there. On investigation he found that it far surpassed in beauty and splendor everything of the kind he had seen up to that time.

Another German sojourning in London in this summer of 1782 was Christoph Friedrich Heinrich Lindemann (1749-1816), who also describes his travels in a very readable book.[8] Lindemann is an independent spirit who goes his own way instead of following the well beaten tracks of his numerous fellow countrymen who wrote on foreign lands. He was in turn chaplain to the Hanoverian troops in Minorca, pastor

[8] *Reisebeschreibungen über einen Theil von Italien, Frankreich und Engelland,* Celle, 1784; by "C. F. H. L.," identified as Lindemann in Holzmann & Bohatta's *Anonymenlexikon.* On Lindemann, see Meusel, *D.G.T.,* Vol. IV, p. 462; Vol. X, p. 210; Vol. XIII, p. 545.

of the garrison church in Lüneburg, and *Superintendent und Pastor* at Lüne in Lüneburg. In treating of England, he knew whereof he spoke, for he had had the opportunity "for seven years of studying the character and the constitution of the English."[9] As a result of his studies, he seems to have come to think more highly of his own people. At any rate he frequently strikes the patriotic note and enjoins the Germans, as Klopstock had long before him (*Mein Vaterland*, 1768), not to forget their own national dignity in their eagerness to grasp and adopt every new feature of foreign civilization.[10] This is a fault, Lindemann observes, with which the English, the French and the Italians could not be charged. Evidence is certainly not wanting to show that the Englishman of the eighteenth century was inclined to look down upon everything foreign.

Evidently Lindemann was in London only during the summer, for it appears that Drury Lane and Covent Garden were closed. To his regret, he was unable to see a Shakespeare tragedy, in which he felt sure that "the English language and English actors would appear truly great."[11] Like Goldsmith,[12] he preferred French to English actors in comedy. The English seemed to him to lack the adaptability so essential to good comic acting and so natural to French actors. On the other hand, he did not care for French tragedy:[13] "The suave, delicate language of the French was distasteful to me when spoken by great heroes. The actors were compelled to mouth their words in order to render the language pompous." What delighted him most was a performance at the Haymarket of *The Beggar's Opera*. Over the exchange of rôles between the sexes therein he split his sides with laughter. But the clergyman had grave misgivings as to the propriety of painting vice in such pleasing colors. His final verdict on this famous opera is, "charming but dangerous."

[9] *Reisebeschreibungen*, p. 4.
[10] *ibid.*, pp. 3, 89.
[11] *ibid.*, p. 127.
[12] See Gray, *op. cit.*, p. 149.
[13] *Reisebeschreibungen*, p. 92.

Ranelagh he dismissed with the single word "insufferable."
The unique feature of this little volume is that it was written
with the definite purpose of taking the Germans to task for
their persistent glorification of things foreign.

The decade 1780-1790 produced German accounts of voyages to England in greater abundance than any other, with
1782 as the banner year. Moritz mentions a dinner party in
that summer given at the home of Reinhold Forster's son-in-
law at which Pastor Lindemann and one Reverend Mr.
Spritter were also present. Judged by the company he kept,
this last-named gentleman might be suspected of the authorship of an anonymous and altogether uninspired work describing a visit to England in 1782.[14] One wonders if the host
may not have mentioned Forster's occupation with the subject, and thereby put the idea into the heads of his three
guests. As a contemporary critic pointed out,[15] this unidenti-
fied writer seems to have borrowed quite freely from the
guide-books. He adds little but volume, and not a great deal
of that, to the travel literature on England. Of all his experiences on the journey he writes with most feeling concerning
his seasickness. His impressions of England, though faint,
were on the whole favorable. Although he could find but two
large theaters in London, he discovered that the people were
fond of shows. "Just as every day-laborer is a politician," he
observes,[16] "likewise every tailor or cobbler, and everyone
who is greater or less than these, is a connoisseur of beauty
and sublimity in the theaters." Whoever cares for that sort
of thing will be pleased with the plays to be seen at Drury
Lane and Covent Garden. Scenery, costumes, music, acting,
everything is excellent. "One might say, in fact, that London
is the school of actors. The slightest flaw is always criticized
in the newspapers the next day, or at least suggestions are

[14] *Reise über Holland nach England;* in *Die Reisenden für Länder- und
Völkerkunde,* von zween Gelehrten hrsg., Vol. III, pp. 36-191; Nürnberg,
1789. The "zwêne Gelehrten" are J. G. Cunardi and J. G. F. Papst.
[15] *Versuch einer Litteratur deutscher Reisebeschreibungen,* Prag, 1793,
p. 130.
[16] *Reise,* p. 189.

given as to how improvements might be made here and there."

Karl Philipp Moritz' book was something of a sensation. Among the reverberations of its appearance were two more attempts to fathom the mysteries of England, neither of them very substantial. The first, that of Johann Gabriel Bernhard Büschel (1758-1813), is itself more or less a mystery. The continuator of Moritz' *Anton Reiser,* Klischnig, says that Büschel was never in England,[17] but gives no authority for the statement. Little is known of Büschel save that he was a native of Leipzig, where he resided many years as a pensioned *Regimentsquartiermeister,* devoting his time to scribbling. Among his publications are *Schauspiele für die deutsche Bühne,*[18] which include a *Graf von Warwick;* and a number of novels, and dramatic criticisms. He is also credited with the authorship of a work on Great Britain antedating the one he is known to have composed. The earlier volume[19] is little more than a patchwork of quotations from Milton, Pope, Robertson and other English writers, detailed descriptions of art collections, and excerpts from guide-books. Practically the only interest attaching to the book is that it attests to the vogue of Sterne in Germany; for instance, when the author undertakes to copy and improve upon the following familiar passage from the *Sentimental Journey:*[20]

[17] See *Deutsche Literaturdenkmale des 18. und 19. Jahrhunderts,* Vol. XXIII, Berlin, 1885, p. 253.

[18] Leipzig, 1780.

[19] *Bemerkungen auf einer Reise durch verschiedene Theile von England, Schottland und Wales,* aus dem Englischen, nebst Anmerkungen des Uebersetzers, Leipzig, 1781. According to the catalog of the Preussische Staatsbibliothek, "it has been ascertained" that Büschel is the author. The preface is signed "Hamburg, April 30, 1781," pointing away from Büschel; but, of course, the place of composition may have been *fingiert.*

[20] Büschel's version of Mr. Yorick's classification of tourists runs as follows:

1. Scheidekünstler und Tonkünstler
   Naturkundige und Zahnärzte
   Sternseher und Marktschreier
   Dichter und Friseurs

2. Reisende vom Ton
   Kinder aus reichen Häusern

Thus the whole circle of travellers may be reduced to the following heads:

Idle Travellers,
Inquisitive Travellers,
Lying Travellers,
Proud Travellers,
Vain Travellers,
Splenetic Travellers;

Then follow

The Delinquent and Felonious Travellers,
The Travellers of Necessity,
The Unfortunate and Innocent Travellers,
The Simple Traveller.

And last of all, if you please, The Sentimental Traveller (meaning thereby myself), . . .

Büschel's *magnum opus*[21] is described on the title-page as a "Pendant to Professor Moritz' Travels." It is in the form of a diary, the first entry in England appearing under the date June 10, 1783. The author surpasses all competitors in eulogizing England, "whose very name is music to German ears." What other foreign visitors before him had praised, he praises too. Roads and conveyances are the best in the world, the food is excellent, the people, even the customs officials, are pleasant and affable, the English constitution is the "masterpiece of all types of government," but finest of all is the enlightenment, "this idol of our writers. . . . This

Die nächsten Erben von Krankheiten, Titeln und Vorzügen
Verirrte von dem Pferderennen zu Newmarket, von Alamack und St. James
Verschwender, ihre Gläubige verlachend
Dilettanten, den Rand der Kenntnisse für eine gaffende Welt abschäumend

3. Reisende aus Zwang, die ihrer Gesundheit wegen ausserhalb Landes gehen, und
Empfindsame Reisende, welche nach Glücklichkeit suchen, und der Wohltat geniessen, wo sie dieselbe finden können.

[21] *Neue Reisen eines Deutschen nach und in England im Jahre 1783,* Berlin, 1784.

gift of the gods is found here, and, I am inclined to say, here alone."[22]

In neither volume does this dramatist and dramatic critic have much to say on the theaters. In the first treatise[23] he observes that "the works of the stage are not all above criticism, although the true *vis comica* has recently been introduced with marked ingenuity by some of our [that is, English][24] dramatic writers." In his second and greater book he describes a visit to "the former country house of Garrick at Hampton Court,"[25] and expresses his admiration for the Hamlet costume, "with broad folds around the neck of the shirt, and wide open breast, which was once introduced into Germany, but fell into disfavor." As he was a summer visitor, he found to his regret that Drury Lane and Covent Garden were closed, but he went to the Little Theatre in the Haymarket, where he experienced the one great disappointment of his journey.[26] He was not comfortably seated, and besides, "the boisterousness of the English, or rather of the English riff-raff, appears here at its worst in all sorts of noise and rude behavior." He describes Vauxhall, Ranelagh, Royal Circus, Bedlam, the hanging of the famous engraver Ryland, and other sights he saw; but despite his efforts to imitate Moritz, he fails to rise above the level of colorless commonplaces.

On reading Moritz, Joachim Friedrich Lehzen[27] was reminded of happy times and pleasant associations in London and felt called upon to take up his pen and emendate that writer. In Moritz' place, he declared, he would never have published those letters, for their subjectivity was in wretched taste.[28] He reviews Moritz' work systematically, revising it

22 *Neue Reisen,* p. 51.
23 *Bemerkungen,* p. 12.
24 As stated above, this work is passed off as a translation.
25 *Neue Reisen,* p. 155.
26 *ibid.,* p. 164.
27 Lehzen was born in 1735; date of death unknown.
28 *Anmerkungen und Erinnerungen über Herrn Professor Moritzens Briefe aus England,* von einem Deutschen, der auch einmal in England gewesen ist, an Herrn L. G-e in Berlin, Göttingen, 1785; see p. 4.

to the greater glory of England and to the author's shame, especially for his slips in the English language. It pained Lehzen, for instance, to read "pickle-salmon" instead of "pickled-salmon." He felt doubly responsible for Moritz, since he too was a Hanoverian. Both he and Lindemann were products of Göttingen,[29] hence in part their attachment to England. Lehzen was assistant pastor of the Marktkirche in Hanover and subsequently pastor in Celle.[30] Since his purpose was only to defend England against Moritz' inconsiderate pen, he discusses no English institutions systematically. He does have something to say about German translations from the English, most of which he deems execrable.[31] Colman's *The jealous Wife* he considers one of the few exceptions. This excellent play, he says, was translated by a man who knew what he was about;[32] but he then proceeds to show how even Bode's rendition could be improved. Lehzen had lived some three years in England and undoubtedly knew his English.

Archenholz alone wrote more pages on the subject of Great Britain than Karl Gottlob Küttner (1755-1805). Lewes says in his *Life of Goethe*,[33] "A certain Küttner, in publishing his *Characters of German Poets and Prose Writers* (1781), could complacently declare that the shouts of praise which intoxicated admirers once raised for Goethe were no longer heard." In so declaring, "Gentle Küttner," as Wieland calls him, erred only in respect to his complacency; for the "shouts of praise" evoked by *Götz von Berlichingen* and *Werther* were never heard again in Goethe's lifetime, not

[29] "Joachim Friedrich Lehzen ist am 14. 4. 1755 als Student der Theologie an der hiesigen Universität immatrikuliert worden, seine Heimat war Bergen b/Lüneburg. Christoph Friedrich Heinrich Lindemann wurde ebenfalls als stud. theol. am 2. 5. 1767 hier immatrikuliert, er stammte aus Erzen." Letter from the Sekretariat, Georg August-Universität, Göttingen, July 16, 1935.

[30] *Das gelehrte Teutschland*, Vol. IV, p. 395; Vol. X, p. 187.

[31] *Anmerkungen und Erinnerungen*, p. 51.

[32] The translator was Bode; see Wihan, J., *Johann Joachim Christoph Bode als Vermittler englischer Geisteswerke in Deutschland*, Prag, 1906.

[33] Everyman's Library, p. 279.

even for *Hermann und Dorothea.* Küttner had studied at
Leipzig, the university second only to Göttingen in cultivating
cultural relations with England. In fact, as the century ad-
vances, Hanover and Saxony stand out more and more as
the regions most susceptible to English influence, replacing
Hamburg and Zürich as the chief German centers of English
culture. Küttner was private tutor to young men in Switzerland, England and Ireland. After many years of residence
and travel abroad, he returned to Leipzig, where he lived
on a pension granted him by the generosity of his former
pupils.[34] His monumental work on England appeared 1791-
1796.[35] It was preceded in 1785 by *Briefe über Irland,* and
followed by a volume on the economic and political condition
of England, and by articles on English culture in the *Hal-
lische Zeitung* and the *Allgemeine Deutsche Bibliothek.* His
books were intended especially for tourists. He borrows
freely from Volkmann, Archenholz and Wendeborn, and
also cites Watzdorf.

Although Küttner's chief work on England did not begin
to appear until 1791, the letters composing it go back to the
year 1783, and it is the theater of that period that he discusses. The *Sentimental Journey* is cited on the first page,
but little of Sterne's influence is traceable in the 2324 pages
following. It is not easy to ascertain this author's personal
views. He either had no strong convictions or preferred to
avoid positive statements. He writes in a loose, rambling
style and does not hesitate to take both sides of a question.
Yet he does disclose his preference for England over other
foreign countries. He is another of the comparative observ-

[34] Thus, the article on K. in the *A.D.B.*; J. G. Burkhard in his *Voll-
ständige Geschichte der Methodisten* (1795, Vol. II, p. 18) says that the
Irish lord in whose home K. was tutor for many years pensioned him.
Burkhard also mentions Hüttner (see below, p. 158, n. 100) and Nitsch as
Germans who had "made their fortune" as private tutors in England.

[35] *Beyträge zur Kenntnis vorzüglich des Innern von England und seiner
Einwohner,* 16 vols., Leipzig, 1791-1796.

The later work is: *Ueber den ökonomischen und politischen Zustand
von Grossbritannien zu Anfang des Jahres 1796,* Leipzig, date of publication
not given.

ers, such as Pöllnitz and Archenholz, and England usually
comes out ahead in the frequent comparisons. Contrary to
the general view of widely travelled men in those days, he
even considered London "a very beautiful city, certainly so
at least in comparison with Paris."[36] He spent the winter
1783-1784 in Manchester and writes of the theater there,[37]
which had the reputation of being one of the best outside
London. It was small, "scarcely larger than the old frame
theater in Leipzig, yet warm and comfortable and exceedingly attractive." Scenery, curtains and stage machinery were
"really good." The actors were "on the whole rather good
than mediocre." Tragedy was given more than comedy, "because not only those here, but English actors in general represent the former better than the latter." It was easier for the
actor to conceal deficiencies behind pomp and rhetoric than
to portray the cultured gentleman in high comedy. In several
respects French provincial troupes, of which Küttner had
seen seven or eight, surpassed the Manchester company. The
French actors, for instance, knew how to dress in contemporary style and to represent the taste and manners of good
society, whereas the Manchester "dandies and gallants" were
often grotesquely dressed, were devoid of good taste, and
unacquainted with the ordinary forms of polite intercourse.
While the actresses scored higher on these points, they still
left much to be desired; so that the spectator was sometimes
compelled to consult the *dramatis personae* to inform himself whether a certain personage was the lady or the lady's
maid. The superiority of tragic to comic acting was due in the
final analysis, however, to the excellence of English tragedies,
"which are at a height unattained by any other nation,"
while French comedies were the greatest. English actors spoke
more slowly than French, hence the English stage was an
excellent language school for the foreigner. They were certainly virtuosos at dying:

[36] *Beyträge*, Vol. I, p. 26.
[37] For Küttner on English theaters, see *Beyträge*, Vol. II, pp. 19-43.

Even the second rate actor cuts a better figure than our best *diers* in Germany. . . . Familiar with all the symptoms of death, they do not look about for a chair or sofa in order to die in a stately manner, but simply fall on the floor, often with such force that one feels concerned about their limbs. One actress in particular reproduced the last frenzied cry of the dying with such horrible realism and several times made such sounds as to cut me to the quick, so that I veritably shuddered. In the tragedy *Isabella* she appears in the fifth act as an insane woman, and never have I seen an impersonation that was so realistic and terrifying.[38] She is not like the dainty French woman, unwilling to lay aside her decorum (*Artigkeit*). No, she appears with the genuine pallor of death, with her hair really dishevelled and her clothing in dire disorder. Her laughter and certain tones of her voice are truly harrowing, arousing unpleasant, distressing feelings. But the English, in this respect as in many others, favor truthfulness to nature.

But such realism does not meet with Küttner's approval. He declares himself in favor of the principle summed up tersely by Voltaire: "Mon cue est dans la nature, et cependant je porte des culottes"; and he was opposed to the naturalistic peasant scenes in *Götz von Berlichingen*. Yet he holds that Garrick went too far in stripping Shakespeare's plays of their "crudities."

Plays of Shakespeare were to be seen almost every week in Manchester. Küttner discusses presentations of *Hamlet* and *Richard III* at length. He was shocked to see farcical elements introduced into the grave-diggers' scene. When one of the grave-diggers removed his ten or twelve waistcoats one by one before setting to work, while the gallery shrieked with laughter, and then actually dug up five skulls and a heap of miscellaneous bones, poor Küttner was thoroughly disgusted. But when Hamlet finally examined Yorick's skull with the comment, "And smell so? puh!", the Continental

---

[38] The actress in question was doubtless Mrs. Siddons. Küttner does not confine himself to a discussion of the Manchester stage.

visitor was sickened. Since the grave was on the proscenium and could not be concealed by the curtain, a stage hand came out before the eyes of the public, swept all the skulls and bones back into the grave, replaced the boards, covered them with a rug and went his way. "The English can stomach such things without taking the slightest offense." The performance of *Richard III,* presumably also in Manchester, was excellent. The actor in the title-rôle was able to portray Richard's hypocrisy in all its nuances. Brückner and Eckhof had both played the part well, "but neither of them understood the real English Richard, who appeared neither in Brückner's elegant attire nor in the red uniform worn by Eckhof, but true to Shakespeare's and the historians' portrait, with a crooked back, a growth on his right shin, heavy black eyebrows and a black wig, and with his whole figure somewhat stooped." He wore "the costume of the period, which was in the old Spanish style." Far from appearing outré, he was marked by a "certain awesome dignity in which the man of power and daring as well as the scoundrel was to be seen." A drawback to Shakespeare performances in the provinces was that they demanded a large number of actors, so that all who were killed in the earlier acts had to be revived for later appearances.

Küttner regretted that English comedy had not even yet been cleansed of the immorality which characterized it in the reign of Charles II. The "groben Sünder" Dryden, Otway and Congreve had unfortunately left their stamp upon the stage. Especially interesting are Küttner's ideas on dramatic verse. It was seldom, he observed, that a French actor could declaim his alexandrines without calling attention to their scansion:

> Blank verse, on the contrary, sounds like poetic prose, and I must pay close attention in the theater if I wish to hear that it is verse. And yet this language has infinitely more charm than prose, not only for the reader but for the theater public. It seems to me that the iambic is the real language of tragedy, and I wonder that it has never been able to take a firm hold in Germany.

These are significant words, since they were written in 1784, at the very time when Goethe and Schiller, encouraged by the recent example of Lessing in *Nathan der Weise,* were engaged in the composition of plays that were to establish iambic pentameter as the standard form for German drama.

In the opinion of this critic the English repertoire was weak not only in comedy, but in the other lighter types of plays as well; yet light afterpieces of some sort were always presented. One of the most popular at the time was Fielding's *Tom Thumb,* but the satire in this little piece was in Küttner's estimation too exaggerated for a second hearing to be bearable. There were scarcely ten English operettas that were "long enough and good enough to be performed as the main piece." Mrs. Brooke's *Rosina* was an exception. It was, in fact, "the best entertainment to be found."

The gallery occupants in Manchester as in London were addicted to rowdyism. Some gentlemen of Küttner's acquaintance saw to it that their ladies occupied the front row of the box, for the ruffians showed some consideration for the fair sex, usually aiming their apple-peels, orange-peels, nutshells and bottles in another direction. As in London, too, there was exemplary order after the performance began.

Küttner gives a long description of Vauxhall,[39] comparing it favorably with the Vauxhall of Milan. In the London place of amusement the crowds were remarkably orderly. "In France there would be guards throughout such a place. . . . In Germany there would soon be fights where the different classes intermingled so. Here there is no supervision, yet no one speaks or laughs loudly."

Not much is known of Heinrich Maximilian Friedrich von Watzdorf (1753-1827?). His account of his sojourn in England, apparently his one literary effort, shows him to have been an amiable gentleman, quite as gentle as his fellow Saxon, Küttner. He was a native of Meissen and served as

[39] *Beyträge,* Vol. I, pp. 19ff.

an officer in the Saxon army,[40] and had travelled in France
and apparently also in Italy before visiting England.[41] His
travel letters are intentionally subjective, falling into the
category of "sentimental journeys." Sterne is mentioned,[42]
and Moritz' influence is discernible. Watzdorf was in England during the summer and autumn of 1784 and, like Moritz,
extended his travels into the country. For his little book
Archenholz wrote an introduction in which he says that the
author had spent but a short time in England, but that "his
thorough knowledge of the English language and his proficiency in speaking it facilitated greatly his efforts in making
the acquaintance of Englishmen and in gaining their confi-
dence," and adds that his own views as set forth in his *England und Italien* are confirmed by the pages that follow. Watzdorf may be said to mark a turning-point in the history of
anglomania in Germany. While he is himself as great an
Englandschwärmer as any of his forerunners, he is con-
sciously writing against a somewhat hostile attitude towards
England which he has encountered in Germany and which
becomes more pronounced as the century wanes. The Britisher, Watzdorf observes, is not "the quiet, serious man,
more irascible than gay," that he is said to be. On the contrary, there is more genuine gaiety in England than in
France.[43] Likewise the Englishman is exculpated from the
charge of being inhospitable, so often brought against him
by foreigners:[44] "Everyone who is not well received in this
country has himself to blame." Contrary to the general impression, the Englishman was affable and polite, far more
so than the Frenchman. The only respect, in fact, in which

[40] See *Das gelehrte Teutschland,* Vol. VIII, p. 355; Vol. IX, p. 366;
Vol. X, p. 791. He is doubtless the General von Watzdorf mentioned by
K. V. von Bonstetten November 21, 1821, as having recently been in
Geneva with the Saxon princes; see *Briefe von Bonstetten an Matthisson,*
hrsg. von H. H. Füssli, Zürich, 1827.
[41] *Briefe zur Charakteristik von England gehörig, geschrieben auf
einer Reise im Jahre 1784,* Leipzig, 1786, pp. 94, 241.
[42] *ibid.,* p. 15.
[43] *ibid.,* p. 70.
[44] *ibid.,* p. 155.

the Englishman is here made to appear less admirable than his neighbor across the Channel is in his greater addiction to alcohol. Intemperate drinking was the curse of the country.[45] A minor vice of the Englishman was his persistent refusal to speak a foreign tongue, even if he had had the advantage of residence abroad.[46] The climax of Watzdorf's journey was his visit to the birthplace of "the immortal Pope," who, rather strangely, looms larger in German *Reisebeschreibungen* than any other English writer of the century.

Watzdorf attended several performances at the Haymarket in the summer, and after his travels through the country found both Drury Lane and Covent Garden open.[47] He was impressed by the spaciousness of the houses, although both were to be replaced within a few years by larger buildings. He considered scenery, costumes and lighting effects magnificent in both theaters. Curiously enough we have heard nothing hitherto on the subject of lights. A feature which appealed to him was the lighting of "the greater part of the boxes," which was avoided in Germany as detracting from the illumination of the stage. But this objection was unwarranted; and flooded with light the pit and the boxes were themselves an impressive spectacle. English actors were "really good." Watzdorf belonged to the small minority who considered comedy superior to tragedy on the London stage. He saw *Hamlet, Lear* and several other tragedies and was of the opinion that the actors had forgotten, "perhaps only since Garrick's death," Hamlet's warnings—that sound advice which is still frequently disregarded in the twentieth century, and not least of all by German actors. In comedy, on the other hand, Watzdorf regards English actors as better than any others he has seen, German, French or Italian. He is aware that this view may seem heretical in Germany, where the image of the Englishman invariably appears with the pistol or the rope by means of which he proposes to end his life.

[45] *Briefe*, p. 94.
[46] *ibid.*, p. 157.
[47] *ibid.*, pp. 239-46, on the theaters.

"But for every one who commits suicide, there are tens of thousands who do nothing but make merry." The comic actors whom Watzdorf most admired were Parsons, the younger Bannister, and Edwin—Parsons in the rôles of comic old men, arrogant noblemen and other caricatures, Bannister as the dandy, or the pompous or timid lover, and Edwin as the fool or clown. They were at their best in *The Merry Wives of Windsor,* in which Parsons took the part of Shallow, Bannister that of Slender, and Edwin that of Hugh Evans. The acting of these three men is described with an enthusiasm equalled only by Lichtenberg in his letters on Garrick. The other parts were also well filled, especially that of Dr. Cajus, a very grateful rôle, since it afforded the welcome opportunity of deriding the Frenchman.

Mrs. Siddons, of course, eclipsed all the other actresses. Watzdorf saw her only in serious drama and wondered whether she also took comic parts. She was great, to be sure, but did not entirely escape the faults common to English tragic acting. He relates the following anecdote from the occasion of her first appearance that season after her return from Dublin:

She not only had had serious misunderstandings with the managers there, but had likewise offended the public. She is generally considered proud and stubborn. When she was on the point of speaking, she was greeted with such mighty hissing and whistling and other signs of displeasure that she could not make herself heard. Many voices cried, "She ought to apologize on her knees !", "She ought to justify her conduct !" At length, after she had been kept for some time in a state of confusion, quiet ensued. Then some one again urged her to "justify her conduct," whereupon she made a little speech in which she did not altogether deny the affair, but excused herself as well as she could, concluding with the words: "After all, if everything were precisely as has been charged against me, I believe every Briton will pardon me when I confess publicly, I am a weak woman." This apology was accepted, the audience applauded and

shouted "Very well!", and she proceeded in the performance of her rôle without the slightest interference.[48]

The only other actress whom Watzdorf singles out for especial praise is Miss Morris, who plays admirably the parts of
"amorous, stubborn and gay girls" at the Haymarket, and
also sings well in light opera.

In his account of the singing of English folk-songs at
Bowling Green and Priesthood Common[49] this visitor intro-
duces a new theme. He was delighted with the songs and
convinced by the beauty of them that the English language,
despite the preponderance of consonants, was quite singable.
Thus this perennial question is once more settled. He was
also charmed by Vauxhall and especially by the English
organ, which he heard there for the first time, and by "the
masterly concert which was given on it." Had he not seen the
instrument, he would have supposed that the music came from
a harmonica, "so soft and sweet was its tone." But the chief
attraction at Vauxhall was the singer Mrs. Kennedy, who
captivated all hearers.

Our good-natured Saxon had no fault to find with the deportment of the public in the places of amusement. At one
time, to be sure, he witnessed the outbreak of a disturbance
in one of the theaters, but it was promptly quelled. For that
matter, he had seen "worse commotions on such occasions at
German universities." But as much could not be said for
Amsterdam, where Watzdorf, though knowing not a word
of Dutch, went with two American friends to the theater

[48] Joseph Knight in his article on Mrs. Siddons in the *Dictionary of
National Biography* gives the following account of the Dublin quarrel:
"She had been openly taxed with taking a large sum of money for acting
in Dublin for the benefit of West Digges, who was in embarrassed circumstances, and for that of Brereton. When seen on 5 Oct. 1784 at Drury
Lane as Mrs. Beverley, she was greeted with loud hissing and a cry of
'Off! Off!' Kemble led her off the stage. She came back, however, and
denied the charges made against her, from which she was vindicated in
the press by a writer signing himself 'Laertes,' supposed to be the
pseudonym of Kemble. From the first charge she is exonerated by Lee
Lewes in his 'Memoirs,' and Brereton somewhat tardily exculpated her
from the second."

[49] *Briefe*, pp. 70, 207.

"just to see the house."[50] But the people were "so ill bred, they scolded, jostled and lambasted one another so" that the sight-seers considered it the part of discretion to give up their efforts and retire from the scene.

Ernst Brandes (1758-1810) was another of the friends of England produced by Göttingen. His father, Georg Friedrich Brandes, had himself absorbed the influences of the Hanove-rian university and had subsequently become still more *eng-lischgesinnt* through a long and profitable residence in Eng-land. On returning to Germany he settled in Hanover as a government functionary and was for many years in charge of the affairs of the university. He was a broadly cultured man. His most intimate friends were the distinguished phi-lologist, Heyne, who was his son-in-law, and Winckelmann. During the Seven Years' War and afterwards his home was a center for Englishmen sojourning in Germany, and both English and French were household languages. Ernst Bran-des studied law at Göttingen from 1775 to 1778, but he must have been there still earlier, for he is mentioned by the Prus-sian Minister Freiherr vom Stein as one of a group of young men with English leanings whom he joined there in 1773.[51]

Ernst Brandes was the author of important works on phil-osophical, educational and political subjects. His earliest ab-sorbing interest, however, was the theater. In 1780-1781 he travelled in France and Germany, devoting his attention mainly to the theaters of Paris and Vienna, on which he con-tributed an article to Boie's *Deutsches Museum*.[52] Likewise during his stay in England, 1784-1785, his avocation at least

[50] *Briefe,* p. 17.

[51] *Lebenserinnerungen von Karl Freiherr von Stein,* Hagen, 1901, p. 7: Im Herbst 1773 besuchte ich mit einem Hofmeister Göttingen, wo ich . . . sehr ernsthaft Jurisprudenz studierte, zugleich aber auch mit der Englischen Geschichte, ihren statistischen, ökonomischen und politischen Werken mich bekannt machte, und überhaupt durch den Umgang mit mehreren gleichgesinnten jungen Männern als Rehberg, Brandes meine Vorliebe für dieses Volk sich befestigte.—Stein himself made a "mine-ralogische und technologische Reise" to England, November 1786-August 1787.

[52] *Bemerkungen über Pariser und Wiener Theater,* 1781.

was the theater. But here he made the acquaintance of Edmund Burke, who became especially interested in him and steered him into the career of publicist, which he followed for the rest of his life.[53] He was secretary of the Hanoverian chancellery and in 1791 succeeded his father in the administration of the affairs of the university. He was a leader in the opposition to the wave of enthusiasm for France which swept over Germany at the outbreak of the French Revolution.[54] His political convictions were derived largely from English sources, and he remained throughout his life steadfastly attached to England. His was not, however, the blind devotion of the German youth of a slightly earlier vintage to an England where "erlaubt ist, was gefällt," as the hero of Goethe's *Torquato Tasso,* a convalescent *Stürmer und Dränger,* pictured the imaginary land of his longings until he was able to grasp to some degree the spirit of a more orderly world in which "erlaubt ist, was sich ziemt." Brandes was, in fact, one of the first to diagnose the anglomania of the *Sturm und Drang* geniuses,[55] who identified freedom with the right to do as one pleases and looked upon England as the country in which a Rousseauistic state of nature had most successfully resisted the encroachments of civilization. He too admired English freedom, but it was a freedom within enlightened laws based on reason that he sought and to some extent found in England.

Brandes has the distinction of being the first German to write a whole volume primarily on the English theater.[56] His book is of interest not only as a review of the London

[53] See Braune, F., *Edmund Burke in Deutschland,* Heidelberg, 1917, pp. 74-113.

[54] cf. Gooch, G. P., *Germany and the French Revolution,* London, 1920, pp. 82*ff.*

[55] See Brandes, E., *Ueber den politischen Geist Englands,* Berlinische Monatsschrift, 1786, p. 115; cf. Elsasser, R., *Ueber die politischen Bildungsreisen der Deutschen nach England,* Heidelberg, 1917, pp. 63*ff.*

[56] *Bemerkungen über das Londoner, Pariser und Wiener Theater,* Göttingen, 1786; pp. 1-233, *Ueber den Zustand der englischen Bühnen, nebst eingestreuten Bemerkungen über das französische und deutsche Theater,* an die Herren G. C. S. und F.; pp. 234-355, a reprint of *Bemerkungen über das Pariser und Wiener Theater.*

theatrical season 1784-1785, but for the sidelights it gives
on the stage in Germany and France, and as a comparative
study in national characteristics. It is as loosely put together
as Lessing's *Hamburgische Dramaturgie,* which obviously
served the writer in a general way as a model. This formless-
ness together with the wide range and great variety of subjects discussed precludes giving here a résumé of the entire
contents. In the beginning the author announces that he will
"from time to time make extensive apparent digressions on
the language, the social tone and the social philosophy, which
on further inspection will be found to be closely connected
with the main theme. It is surprising," he adds,[57] "to what
a great extent the comedies of a nation portray the social
customs." He hesitates to follow in Lichtenberg's steps as a
critic of the London stage, but in the decade since the famous
Garrick letters were written many changes have occurred.
—"Garrick is no more, and Mrs. Siddons was not." Brandes
would divide English drama into two halves, "placing Shakespeare on the one side and everything else on the other." It is
customary, he observes, to identify the English theater with
its greatest figure. "If the French mean Shakespeare, they
say *les Anglais,* or *le Théâtre anglais.*"[58] He seems inclined
likewise to look upon Mrs. Siddons as one-half of the contemporary scene, for he devotes some fifty pages to her and
but little more to all other English actors combined.

As a dramatic critic Brandes treats us with an occasional
surprise, but, if we make the allowances necessary for any
appraiser of the works of his contemporaries, we find that his
judgment is usually sound. Deprived of the perspective of
distance, the best critics frequently go wrong. In the present
case the *Barbier de Séville* and *Le mariage de Figaro,* two
out of the small number of plays from that period that were
destined to live, come in for wholesale condemnation. Brandes cannot understand why these dull pieces have found such
great favor in Germany, but is forced to ascribe their popu-

[57] *Bemerkungen,* p. 8.
[58] *ibid.,* p. 75.

larity to the *estime de parole* for everything that passes muster in Paris.[59] The lack of good German comedies, our critic holds, finds its explanation in the language itself, which, owing to the still general use of French in polite intercourse, has never developed the lighter tone. "Wir sind für Gedanken, nicht für Töne gemacht."[60] But the German language had in it the seed of the greatest elegance, as Brandes was convinced on reading Zimmermann's *Einsamkeit,* which was to him a linguistic revelation.[61] Germany could boast of but one great comedy, *Minna von Barnhelm,* "a masterpiece, so far as the comic element is concerned." But Lessing's forte was tragedy. He could never quite succeed in the portrayal of female characters in comedy.[62] A footnote just here adds nothing to the writer's reputation as a critic:

> Schröder has shown conclusively in his *Ring,* an adaptation to German taste of Farquhar's *Constant Couple,* and in the character of Franziska in his *Victorine* that we Germans may have polite comedy. *Der Vetter von Lissabon* [also by Schröder] is the best drama that any nation can point to.

Previously Brandes had declared that Diderot's *Père de famille* was the play dearest to his heart. Of it he writes: "If the theater can make men better, which is extremely doubtful, . . . it is only by means of such plays." His judgment of Sheridan has been better sustained by posterity. Evidently disregarding the Shakespeare half of the theater, he pronounces *The School for Scandal* "the most excellent comedy that the English have." He rated *The Rivals* far below it. Incidentally he considered the performance of *The School for Scandal* the finest of the whole season in London.[63] Colman's *Jealous Wife* and *Clandestine Marriage,* both well known in Germany, were among the best and at the same time the

---

[59] *Bemerkungen,* p. 15.

[60] *ibid.,* p. 30.

[61] Brandes himself is recognized as a reformer of the German language; see article on him in the *A.D.B.*

[62] *Bemerkungen,* p. 31.

[63] *ibid.,* p. 55.

"most decent" English comedies.[64] In comparison with Sheridan and Colman, Cumberland and Murphy were second rate. Murphy's plays, like those of his contemporaries in general, are not so immoral as the older comedies. Yet in *The Way to keep Him* "there is a scene in which the lackey kisses the chambermaid, which would scarcely pass in Germany, because it is too true to nature."[65] Garrick's afterpieces receive some praise from this critic, though *High Life below Stairs* is included among them by mistake.[66] This little comedy proved to be quite delightful, with Bannister as Lord Duke, Palmer as the lord's servant, and Miss Pope as Kitty. Garrick's *Bon Ton, or High Life above Stairs,* was known in Germany in a rather poor translation as *Guter Ton,*[67] and, despite the free and easy spirit of it, had been well received there. "This is proof," he argues, as Lessing had when this young critic was in his cradle, "that our taste in drama is much closer to the English than to the French, and that we can stand for a great deal more."[68]

Literary critics would do well to refrain from prophecy. Brandes was convinced that Foote's comedies would maintain themselves forever on the stage because of "the astonishing truth and the knowledge of human nature, which are often brought out in a few words and which convince everyone that they [the plays] were stolen from nature."[69] Echoing Lessing on Shakespeare, he continues: "In him [Foote] is the genuine art of Molière. He does not tell us what people are like, he shows them to us." Like Küttner, Brandes deplored the lax morality of many English comedies and ascribed a good part of the blame to Charles II. In recent

[64] *Bemerkungen,* p. 41.

[65] *ibid.,* p. 59.

[66] The author is Townley.

[67] The only translation listed by Price, M. B., & Price, L. M., in *The Publication of English Literature in Germany in the Eighteenth Century* (Univ. of Calif. Press, 1934, p. 66) is *Der Ton der grossen Welt,* translated by C. G. Harold, Altenburg, 1776. The play is by Colman and Garrick.

[68] *Bemerkungen,* p. 41.

[69] *ibid.,* p. 37.

times certain Germans, "among others Herr Wetzel,"[70] had attempted to introduce "English license" on the German stage, but the manner in which it was done had provoked opposition. Brandes, for his part, strongly disapproves of German imitations of "English license." He considers German adaptations of English plays generally unsatisfactory and finds the explanation in the plays themselves. English comedies are the most difficult of all to transplant to foreign soil, because the morals therein, instead of being derived from real characters, are usually based upon "compendium principles" and expressed in pedantic platitudes. Grasping a psychological tenet more familiar to our times than to his, this discerning student of human nature believes that the English commonly err in making the vain attempt to uproot dominant evil traits instead of directing evil towards good in normal character development. "It is really strange," he says,[71] "that this nation, superior in so many respects to all others, is in this respect so very backward."

The treatment of the love theme in the comedy of the three countries covered by his study affords Brandes material for interesting reflections. The Frenchman, he finds, delights in charming, gallant little romances embellished by witty conversation. The German ennobles love with a strong admixture of lofty sentiment. But the Englishman, always the true *Naturmensch,* takes nature as he finds it, without French sophistication or German sentimentalism :[72]

> This difference in the manner of loving has an important effect upon the tone of comedies. I believe that the manner peculiar to us Germans is one of the chief reasons why our lovers are such stiff, insufferable creatures on the stage. I am aware at the same time that much depends on the authors, whose lack of familiarity with the tone of polite society is here quite evident. Love in the German manner borders on tragedy and must be

[70] Johann Karl Wezel (1747-1819) ; he had visited England, and was, when B. wrote, *Theaterdichter* in Vienna.
[71] *Bemerkungen,* p. 73.
[72] *ibid.,* p. 20.

kept in the background if the comic element is not to be submerged.

At last the time has come, however, thanks mainly to Lessing, when an unprejudiced critic may reasonably hold up German drama to a comparison with the contemporary works of English and French dramatists. Brandes, if called upon to characterize in a few words the tragic output of the three countries, would say that German tragedy is marked by wisdom and philosophy, as in the case of *Emilia Galotti* or *Julius von Tarent* and their numerous imitations; French tragedy since Voltaire by rhetoric, and English by bombast.[73] He rates Klinger higher than Schiller, who at the time had published three plays. Klinger's *Die Zwillinge* is superior to anything Schiller has written. *Fiesco* in particular is marred by bombast, artificiality and exaggeration, and by "personified passion," which is also the worst fault of French tragedy. No other nation has been so fortunate as the English in their choice of material for tragic treatment. They employ the most dramatic situations and represent the most violent passions. The subject matter is not derived from remote sources such as Greek mythology or ancient history, but is indigenous and usually from the middle ages or even modern times. Consequently English tragedy is "better" on the whole than that of any other nation, and, when well presented, the most effective on the stage. It also affords the actors the best opportunities for the exercise of their talents.[74] But at present the performances are worthy of England's great dramatic literature only when Mrs. Siddons participates in them. Blank verse proves a snare for all but really great actors, beguiling them into a "sort of bombastic declamation which the English call ranting." One of Brandes' prophecies that has been fulfilled is that German drama, freed from alexandrines and the rules of French pseudo-classicism, will soon surpass the English, "Shakespeare excepted." He could not foresee, however, that it would be blank-verse drama and that the author

---

[73] *Bemerkungen*, p. 88.
[74] *ibid.*, p. 96.

of *Fiesco* would develop into the greatest German dramatist.

Brandes has much to say on the subject of Shakespeare,[75] most of which, to be sure, is to be found in earlier German sources. He deplores "all the modern chiselling on the sublimest structure of former times," but thanks heaven that the emendators of Shakespeare's plays no longer venture to make interpolations but restrict themselves to omissions, though unfortunately some of the finest passages are thus suppressed. He regrets that the rôle of Ophelia is assigned in both theaters on the strength of the candidate's accomplishments as a singer, which he considers relatively unimportant; and that the mania for operettas has been allowed to disfigure several of Shakespeare's plays. *The Tempest* had been debased to an opera, and a whole army of witches had been added to the cast of *Macbeth,* so that witches' arias and witches' choruses might be introduced. Though still quite young, Brandes "can remember well when Shakespeare was altogether contraband in at least certain sections of Germany and all who could so much as bear to read him were held in contempt." He doubts furthermore if Lessing's *Hamburgische Dramaturgie* would have won Germany over to the English dramatist without the supplementary propaganda of the *Sturm und Drang* "Schenies."[76] Here, in Brandes' opinion, Goethe's example counted for most. "His *Götz* is in a class by itself," he continues, "and with all my profound admiration for Shakespeare, I still do not believe that he ever produced anything of such coherent perfection." By this he doubtless means—and it is scarcely an overstatement—that no other single work in dramatic form presents such a complete, vivid

---

[75] *Bemerkungen,* pp. 75*ff.*

[76] Brandes here makes a good point. The *Sturm und Drang* writers owe their enthusiasm for the English stage perhaps less to Lessing directly than to Herder and Eschenburg. Lessing, with all his academic admiration for Shakespeare, exercised chiefly a negative influence, in breaking down the prestige of French tragedy, while Herder and Eschenburg had the deeper appreciation of Shakespeare's genius, and besides spoke a language which appealed more strongly to the *Stürmer und Dränger* than Lessing's rationalism. Cf. Gundolf, F., *Shakespeare und der deutsche Geist,* VIII. Auflage, Berlin, 1927, pp. 192-3, 198*ff.*

and colorful picture of a whole age. Of English dramatists aside from Shakespeare, Brandes prefers Otway, especially for his *Venice preserv'd.* Then comes Rowe with his *Fair Penitent* and *Jane Shore.* The bombast of Dryden and Lee makes them almost unbearable. The subject matter of Lillo's *George Barnwell* and of Moore's *Gamester* is as admirable as the execution, especially in the case of the latter, is "matt und schwach."

A peculiarity of the London stage is that almost all actors play in both comedy and tragedy. Thus, Brandes argues, the prominent players are too preoccupied with leading rôles to have any time for minor parts, which are accordingly neglected despite their great importance to the effect of the performance as a whole. As we have heard from Archenholz, English actors put others to shame in learning their rôles. Brandes had never known Mrs. Siddons to be guilty of the slightest lapse of memory. "It seems as if Germany were the home of poor memorizing," he laments.[77] He also concurs in the general praise for the mechanical side of English theatrical art. The machinery in both houses is extraordinarily good and the settings by far the best he has ever seen, "not gaudy opera decorations, but realistic reproductions of the actual scenes."[78] For this reason English pantomimes are the best, in fact, the only ones worth seeing. Contrary to the usual opinion of foreign visitors, Brandes sees nothing remarkable in the costumes on the London stage, though Drury Lane impresses him more favorably in this respect than Covent Garden. The infallible Mrs. Siddons alone shows the taste in dress which is the rule on the Paris stage. The Danish courtiers in *Hamlet,* for instance, "look precisely as if the purpose had been to make certain small courts appear ridiculous."

None of the tragedians was a match for Schröder. Henderson and Kemble were the best. The former, although his figure counted against him, often attained to greatness in

[77] *Bemerkungen,* p. 229.
[78] *ibid.,* p. 220.

acting. He was at his worst as Theseus in *Phèdre* and at his best as Falstaff. Smith, already past fifty, retained his youthful figure and was of the athletic build seen so frequently on the English stage, but never on the French. He was at times impressive as Macbeth and at least fair enough as Biron in Southerne's *The fatal Marriage*[79] not to spoil the effect of Mrs. Siddons' superb acting. As Lord Hastings in *Jane Shore* he was mediocre, and almost insufferable as Osman in Congreve's *The mourning Bride* and as Athelwold in William Mason's *Elfrida*. He was at his best in comedy, especially as Charles Surface in *The School for Scandal* and as Oakley in the elder George Colman's *The jealous Wife*.[80] Palmer, then in his prime, was, says Brandes, "one of the handsomest English figures I have ever seen, with a large frame, broad shoulders and strong features." In tragedy he was only fair, but in comedy one of the greatest actors of his day, by far the best in England. One of his finest rôles was that of Colonel Feignwell in Mrs. Centlivre's *Bold Stroke for a Wife*.[81] Palmer was the London Molé; the man of the world according to English standards as Molé was according to those of Paris. Kemble reached great heights as Hamlet, far surpassing the German Hamlets this writer had seen, though he adds that he has never seen Brockmann or Schröder in that rôle.[82] King makes a good Lord Oglesby in *The clandestine Marriage*; and "Dodd plays the beaux in the usual English style, that is to say, unbearably overdrawn."

Brandes' enthusiasm for Mrs. Siddons knows no bounds.[83] He is always dissatisfied with himself when he undertakes to discuss her acting, he says, the subject being beyond him. He saw her in all her rôles at least twice and in some of them three or four times. He also "observed her extremely closely and at length" in the drawing room, where in his eyes she was even more fascinating than on the stage. His pen-portrait

[79] i.e., Garrick's adaptation, *Isabella, or the Fatal Marriage.*
[80] *Bemerkungen,* pp. 118*ff.*
[81] *ibid.,* p. 123.
[82] *ibid.,* p. 135.
[83] *ibid.,* 152*ff.*

of Mrs. Siddons seems to belie his professed inability to do justice to the subject. Her beauty is of a type not usually admired in England, where the preference is for "insignificant painted-china faces" (*unbedeutende niedliche Dosengesichter*), nor generally appreciated elsewhere. "She has not the appeal of Tizian's Venus; she speaks only to the soul and the spirit." On the stage she retains nothing of her usual appearance, but is completely transformed into the character she represents. Brandes rated Mme. Sacco the greatest tragic actress he had seen hitherto; but the Viennese artist could not hold a light to Mrs. Siddons, "whom nature herself seems to have equipped for first rank in her art." In nobility of features, in the "power and manifold variety of her facial expression" she was unsurpassable. This German admirer made inquiries of many who remembered Mrs. Woffington, Mrs. Cibber, Mrs. Pritchard, Mme. Dumenil and Mlle. Clairon, and nearly all gave the palm to Mrs. Siddons on "expression of countenance." Her gestures were natural and effective, although she used her arms less than Continental actresses. In dress she "surpassed all French and certainly all German actresses." She usually wore satin, her preference being for black and white, and next in order blue. Her performance as Lady Macbeth taxes our critic's stock of superlatives. The most impressive words he ever heard in the theater were from her lips: "Glamis thou art, and Cawdor, and shalt be what thou art promised." He saw her also as Desdemona, as Belvidera in Otway's *Venice preserv'd,* which was said to be her favorite rôle; as the heroine of "Mason's impotent drama" *Elfrida,* as Zara in *The mourning Bride,* as Jane Shore, as Euphrasia in Murphy's *The Grecian Daughter*, Isabella in *The fatal Marriage,* Lady Randolph in John Home's *Douglas,* Lady Beverley in *The Gamester,* and the Lady of Valori in Cumberland's *The Carmelite*. One performance of *Jane Shore* was enough even for this Siddons devotee. "The sight is terrible," he writes. "I saw two ladies among the spectators fall into hysterics, and one of them had to be carried out, laughing convulsively. . . . Such representations of physical pain are too much for modern nerves." He did not see Mrs. Siddons' Rosalind, but had no desire to see the born tragedian in comedy.

Mrs. Siddons' two sisters, the Misses Kemble, were only fair; Miss Farren and Miss Pope were admirable; Mrs. Crawford, the former Mrs. Barry, had seen her best days; Miss Younge, subsequently Mrs. Pope, was a great actress; and so was Mrs. Abington still, notwithstanding her advanced age. Brandes had the interesting experience of seeing Mme. Adamberger in Vienna, Mme. Dugazon in Paris and Mrs. Abington in London as Roxalna in *The Sultan,* "nach Favart's *Soliman Second.*"[84] Dugazon was the best in this particular rôle.

There is abundance of evidence to prove that the theater audiences in London became more polite towards the end of the century.[85] Brandes speaks a word in their defense, claiming that they are quieter than those of other cities where the police are in control. "Bucks and bloods" who have imbibed too freely are usually responsible for the disturbances that still occur. The common people maintain order not only among themselves, but on the stage as well, for they demand of the performers apologies for any lapses of which they may be guilty and are always ready to accept reasonable satisfaction for their complaints. Furthermore they are sophisticated enough to refrain from laughing during the performance of tragedies on hearing certain words that strike them as amusing, a virtue which the theater public in most German cities had not yet acquired.

The two currents of anglomania, the one arising in the *Aufklärung,* the other in the *Sturm und Drang,* streamed to-

[84] On this point B. is mistaken. Bickerstaffe's *Sultan* is based on Marmontel's *Soliman II* (See *Marmontel's Moral Tales,* ed. by G. Saintsbury, London, 1895, pp. 1*ff.*). *The Sultan* was first performed at Drury Lane December 12, 1775 (See Nicoll, *op. cit.,* pp. 121, 238). Favart's *Les trois Sultanes, ou Soliman Second* was first performed November 8, 1776 (See *Répertoire du Théâtre Français,* ed. by M. Petitot, Paris, 1884, Vol. XXII, p. 157).

[85] See Nicoll, *op. cit.,* p. 130.

gether through the impressionable soul of Sophie von la
Roche (1731-1807).[86] Perhaps the most interesting female
figure in the cultural life of Germany from the time of
Hrosvitha of Gandersheim to her own, the representative
woman of German letters in her century as her granddaughter
Bettina was in the first half of the following, she ran the
whole gamut of intellectual innovations in her day, still
clinging to the old while seizing eagerly upon the new. Once
the fiancée of her cousin, Wieland, and the muse of much of
his early sentimental poetry, Klopstock enthusiast, friend of
Goethe, Merck, Georg Jacobi, Lavater, Basedow, to mention
but a few members of her ever changing inner circle, acquainted with most of the contemporary German and Swiss
littérateurs and with many celebrities in France and England,
this charming Swabian lady was well equipped to preside over
the leading German salon of her day. From the Klopstock cult
she made an easy transition to the school of Rousseau, under
whose influence she devised great plans for the education of
German womanhood. Her first and best novel, *Die Geschichte
des Fräuleins von Sternheim,* the chief German forerunner
of *Werther,* as her *Rosaliens Briefe* was of *Wilhelm Meister,*
shows her devotion to England and English literature, and
especially to Richardson. In 1786[87] Sophie had the great
pleasure of spending forty days in England. Much of her
time must have been devoted to her diary, for it bears the
appearance of having been written day by day on the journey,
and averages more than ten printed pages for each day. First
to last it is English enlightenment that wins her strongest
encomiums and inspires her most extravagant transports.
Her diary, like Moritz' *Travels,* is easily accessible to English readers, having appeared recently in an excellent transla-

[86] Werner Milch's *Sophie la Roche, die Grossmutter der Brentanos,*
Frankfurt, 1935, is a fascinating book and is particularly valuable for the
treatment of Sophie's social and intellectual background.

[87] Not 1787, as stated in her diary and most German references to it, but
1786, as stated by Erich Schmidt in *A.D.B.*

tion,[88] so little need be said here of its general contents. On one point Sophie errs. She says[89] that London and England have always meant more to her than Paris and France. So far, so good. But she adds, "though not so much as Italy." Here she overestimates her emotional resources, for England undoubtedly taxed them to the limit. She was never in Italy, but apparently shared the vague northern yearning for southern skies and marble columns that was in the air she breathed; and besides she had been engaged to an Italian before her betrothal to Wieland. Her diary of her trip to France in 1785 shows no lack of enthusiasm for that country, but she was depressed by the poverty and wretchedness on all sides in Paris and elsewhere in this period of approaching disaster. As the climax of her visit to Paris was her meeting with Madame de Genlis,[90] likewise in London her most precious experience was not her presentation at court, but her introduction to Miss Burney. Since the author of *Evelina* occupied somewhat the same position in English letters as Sophie in German, it would seem that the two ladies should have had much in common. But perhaps the Klopstockian sentimentalism of Sophie's outburst—*Miss Borni! la plus chère, la plus digne des Angloises! dites-moi, m'aimez-vous?*—was too much for Fanny's Anglo-Saxon reserve. At any rate the cool tone of her version of the encounter[91] contrasts sharply with her German admirer's warmth.

Needless to say, Sophie promptly found her way to the theater, especially as she concurred in the general opinion that "a great deal of the national character is always revealed in

[88] *Sophie in London, 1786,* translated by Clare Williams, London, 1933; with an interesting introduction by the translator. The first German edition was *Tagebuch einer Reise durch Holland und England von der Verfasserin von Rosaliens Briefen,* Offenbach, 1788; the second edition, to which references are made below, *Tagebuch einer Reise durch Holland und England von Sophie Witwe von la Roche,* Offenbach, 1791.

[89] *Tagebuch,* p. 193.

[90] See *Journal einer Reise durch Frankreich von der Verfasserin von Rosaliens Briefen,* Altenburg, 1787, pp. 369, 409, 422-35.

[91] *Diary and Letters of Madame d'Arblay,* London, 1892, Vol. II, pp. 170ff.

the playhouses." Since the large theaters were closed, she made for the Haymarket. Her command of the English language was very imperfect, according to her own statement,[92] which is confirmed by Miss Burney.[93] Consequently the performances were little more than pantomimes to her. On her first theater evening she saw three little pieces, all of them quite pleasing. The mountings were especially effective, and the acting of Miss Farren, Mr. Palmer, and a certain twelve-year-old girl, who "deserved to become the darling of the nation," was most excellent. Her second evening was more noteworthy. At last a German sojourning in London may see a German play, for *Minna von Barnhelm* has been running for the past month at the Haymarket in the translation by Johnstone as *The disbanded Officer*. Of this historic event Sophie writes:

> It was on the whole an excellent performance, with Miss Farren as Minna, Palmer as the Major, and Edward (Edwin!) as Just. The house was well filled, and many spectators, even some of the men, were moved to tears by the splendid traits with which the great and noble soul of our Lessing has endowed his creatures. In the excerpt from the criticism of the play Lessing is called the favorite and the Shakespeare of the Germans. The translator confesses that he "was unable to give a perfect rendition, since Lessing's wit, delicacy and beautiful language were not translatable." But people said at the same time that "the contents of this comedy were too scant and meager for the English stage, although warm feelings and noble impulses animated every scene, precluding tedium." Might not one ask, then, "What more do you wish?"

A few weeks later Frau von la Roche was happy to be able to visit Drury Lane, "not only because I was to see the famous Mrs. Siddons perform, but also because I should again see many Englishmen with their families, all of whom

[92] *Tagebuch,* pp. 158, 191.
[93] *Diary and Letters,* Vol. II, p. 176.

I have come to esteem very highly."[94] It goes without saying that she was enraptured by Mrs. Siddons' acting. "There is no greater actress in existence," she declared, "nor any whose figure could be better adapted to noble tragedy. More natural-ness and unstudied grace one can not imagine." Again she had the pleasure of seeing strong men weep, for Mrs. Siddons was giving of her best as Belvidera in *Venice preserv'd*. This time Sophie's tender soul was so stirred that silent weeping seemed inadequate—"man möchte laut weinen."

With the endurance of a Madame de Staël, Frau von la Roche found time between her visits to Warren Hastings, Cagliostro, Lord George Gordon, Herr Forster,[95] Madame la Fite, Miss Burney and Bedlam to make the rounds also of Covent Garden, Saddler's Wells, Royal Circus and Vauxhall. Everywhere she was delighted with the entertainment, but was primarily absorbed in her studies of human nature in the English edition. At Covent Garden, where she saw "a re-markable play called *The Belle's Stratagem*,"[96] she was di-verted by one of the disturbances that still sometimes en-livened English theaters.[97] A man "on almost the highest bench" halted the performance long enough to have an offen-sive neighbor removed from the house, after which the actors proceeded with the play. And all this took place in the presence of the royal family!

In the period 1780-1787 anglomania reaches its height. Throughout all the writings of German travellers during these years, from Moritz to Sophie von la Roche, there flows a steady undercurrent of fervid enthusiasm for everything English—a positive *Englandschwärmerei*. Something of the *Sturm und Drang* spirit characterizes the attitude of the en-

---

[94] *Tagebuch,* p. 508.

[95] The index of the English translation lists J. R. Forster in connec-tion with the references to "Herr Forster"; but they are neither to him nor to his son George, both of whom had for some years been living in Ger-many. The Herr Forster in question was a "Magdeburger," as Sophie states (p. 306).

[96] By Mrs. Cowley.

[97] *Tagebuch,* p. 424.

tire group, not excepting Ernst Brandes, who has on the whole little admiration for the young "geniuses" of his generation. And it is more than a mere coincidence that anglomania begins to subside in Germany about the time when the *Sturm und Drang* has run its course. In practically all these writers, and especially in Moritz, something of Sterne's influence is discernible, and while the attempts to imitate the *Sentimental Journey* are not always successful, they do in general result in imparting a bit of sprightliness and charm to a type of literature that had hitherto been for the most part colorless in style.

As for the drama, Shakespeare had already been elevated to the pinnacle which he has ever since occupied in Germany. Not one of these writers questions English preeminence in the field of modern tragedy, though Küttner, like many other critics then and since, prefers French to English comedy. Despite the decline of the London stage, German visitors still found a number of actors worthy of their admiration. Watzdorf is the first to mention Mrs. Siddons by name, and from 1784 on this incomparable actress claims as much attention from German visitors to England as Garrick had in his day. Staging and scenic effects are generally praised, and the audience, while still given to occasional boisterous demonstrations before the play begins, are described as exemplary in their orderliness and attentiveness when it is once under way.

CHAPTER IV

CRITICAL VISITORS

FEW Germans in the eighteenth century had better opportunities for becoming acquainted with English life than
Gebhard Friedrich August Wendeborn (1742-1811). Aside
from two trips to France and occasional visits to Germany,
Switzerland and Holland, he spent nearly twenty-five years
in England. He had prepared for the ministry at Halle and
Helmstedt and continued his candidacy under the redoubtable
Pastor Goeze in Hamburg. In 1768 he became pastor of the
new German church in Ludgate Hill, which owed its origin
to a schism in St. Mary's in Savoy. This position he held
until 1790. Thanks to the degree of Doctor of Laws, con-
ferred on him by the University of Edinburgh, he was able
to style himself "Doktor Wendeborn." By Christian Daniel
Ebeling, the editor of his memoirs, Wendeborn is accredited
with having awakened the interest of Englishmen in the
study of the German language.[1] With hopes of an appoint-
ment as teacher of German to the Prince of Wales, he published in 1774 his *Elements of the German Language,* which
reached its seventh edition in 1819. His views and reflections
on England, not conspicuously original or interesting, are
spread over hundreds of pages in three main works and a
number of articles.[2] Like Volkmann and Küttner, he wrote

[1] *Wendeborn, Erinnerungen aus seinem Leben,* Hamburg, 1813, Introduction, p. iv.

[2] *Beiträge zur Kenntnis Grossbritanniens vom Jahre 1779,* anon., hrsg.
von George Forster, Lemgo, 1780.

*Der Zustand des Staats, der Religion, der Gelehrsamkeit und der Kunst
in Grossbritannien gegen das Ende des 18. Jahrhunderts,* 4 vols., Berlin,
1784-1788; translated under the author's supervision as *A View of England
towards the close of the Eighteenth Century,* 2 vols., London, 1791.

Reise durch einige Provinzen Englands, Hamburg, 1793.

1779-1792 W. was London correspondent of the *Hamburger Correspondent.*

with the interests of travellers in mind, frequently employing the guide-book style. While lacking the enthusiasm of the *Stürmer und Dränger,* he was on the whole an ardent admirer of England, and especially of the English "national character," which he attempted to analyze in some fifty pages. But, like Archenholz, he fancied that he saw the erstwhile great nation gradually undergoing a change for the worse, and by 1790 he too was almost completely turned against Great Britain.

On the English theaters, of which he wrote in the year 1787,[3] Wendeborn expresses himself with more reserve than usual, disclaiming the qualifications of the dramatic critic. Although he had frequently attended the theater in Paris and knew the London stage well, he was not willing to venture an opinion on the ever recurring question as to which of the two was the greater. While observing that Lord Chesterfield regarded the French stage as the greatest in the world,[4] he reveals plainly enough his own preference for the English. Sharing to some extent Sophie von la Roche's Rousseauistic views on education, Wendeborn considered the English educational system the best, since it held to the same spirit of freedom and the same regard for nature that was reflected in English gardens. The Englishman "loves nature"; he writes,[5] "he comes to her aid again and again with a helpful hand, he will not allow art to destroy any of her works. This very trait accounts for the Englishman's attaining most nearly to the real dignity and destiny of man." And this admirable trait also characterizes the dramatic works of the English, which show "somewhat the same taste as their gardens." Though recognizing the importance of "unity of action," Wendeborn feels that dramatic rules should not be taken too seriously. He has often heard that tragedy appeals more strongly to the English taste than comedy. This is no

[3] *Zustand,* etc., Vol. IV, pp. 424-62.
[4] See *The Letters of Philip Dormer Stanhope, Earl of Chesterfield,* 3 vols., London, 1892, Vol. I, p. 372; "There is not, nor ever was, any theater comparable to the French." (November 8, O. S., 1750.)
[5] *Zustand,* etc., Vol. II, p. 239.

longer the case, he declares, for "there are now certainly twice as many comedies written as tragedies." Scenery and costumes are as a rule "beautiful and expensive," and the music is usually good. The moral tone of the stage has gradually improved during the past century, "although many slippery and ambiguous expressions are still tolerated." But even the female element of the audience seems to be shock-proof.

Generally speaking, Wendeborn found "the declamation good and the acting natural" on the English stage. He had the privilege of seeing both Garrick and Mrs. Siddons many times. He considered Garrick the greatest actor he had ever seen; but for reasons not stated he thinks Mrs. Siddons is very much overrated, owing her reputation in part to a good press. The veteran Mrs. Abington is still "one of the best actresses." Both actors and playwrights reap rich financial rewards. "Mrs. Inchbald received 705 pounds sterling in the winter of 1786 for her mediocre comedy *Such Things are.* Hence it is worth while to compose a play." Foote, who was formerly called the English Aristophanes, is falling into oblivion. Of his pieces, once so popular, only *The Devil upon two Sticks* is still alive on the stage. Dr. Wendeborn deals severely with Foote. He holds that "the English Aristophanes" had little besides coarseness and licentiousness in common with his great namesake. Foote spared not even his friends and benefactors, for example, "good old Glover," whom he handled quite roughly. He deserved nothing better himself than to be "in Footischen 'Wolken' durchgezogen."

Although we hear less and less about disorder in the playhouses, Wendeborn does observe, like so many before him, that the "English show their vaunted freedom nowhere more than in the theaters." Here, he says, "aristocrats and commoners are gathered, and the latter are bent on showing that they consider themselves quite as good as the former. . . . The upper gallery controls the whole house, even the actors being compelled to obey orders." It is especially gratifying to this democratic onlooker to see how responsive "the gods in the upper gallery" are to the beauties of the plays. He does not mar the picture by suggesting that the applause is in some cases ordered and paid for in advance by the author or his friends. And far from being shocked by the irreverence of the people, this future partisan of the French revolutionists notes with satisfaction that the audience also has the King well in hand. If he comes late, instead of being hailed with applause, he is greeted with tokens of disapproval, whereupon he looks at his watch and shakes his head. On the strength of this pantomime apology he is given his little ovation.

Wendeborn makes some interesting comments on the repertoire of the theaters. If a Shakespeare play is produced, it must be brilliantly staged, and interspersed with songs, dances and other divertissements between the acts in order to keep the audience awake. "Those in Germany who, often because they know no better, worship Shakespeare even more than the English do, will certainly be surprised to hear this; but it is nevertheless the absolute truth. I have seen various Shakespeare plays performed before audiences which were conspicuously bored, although a Garrick or a Woodward employed his talents to make them pleasing." This iconoclast is of the opinion that Voltaire, while too severe, was not altogether wrong in his criticism of the English dramatist, and that the German Shakespeare worship has been overdone. He is also in a position to put his fellow countrymen right on another point. Having seen Addison's *Cato* played "at least three times" before very small houses, he had convinced himself that it was the soporific effect of the piece and not, as he had often heard in Germany, its tendency to aggravate the well known English proclivity to suicide that accounted for its being seldom given. "I saw the spectators yawn," he says, "but I did not see them fall into fits of melancholy." As for the performance of Lessing's comedy, Wendeborn writes:

A German play had never been given on the London stage until last year, when Lessing's *Minna von Barnhelm* was played at the Little Theatre in the Haymarket in a much altered version as *The disbanded Officer,* but it survived not a dozen performances.

Although the first attempt to introduce a German play in London met with poor success, it nevertheless marks the beginning of a new era in the literary relations between the two countries. By the end of the century Germany is repaying part of her debt to England in the form of dramatic works, of which the most popular were those of Kotzebue and Iffland. German visitors were naturally interested in the reception of these importations, and frequently mentioned the subject, as we shall see. However, not only Kotzebue and Iffland, but Schiller as well, found greater favor with the English reading public than with the theater audiences.

The travel letters of Jacob Christian Gottlieb Schaeffer (1752-1826) represent a special point of view. The author, the first Bavarian among our tourists, was personal physician to the Prince of Thurn and Taxis, and became widely known for his writings on children's diseases and other medical subjects. Together with one Baron von Eberstein he accompanied the two sons of the prince on an extensive European tour. The party spent the winter of 1787 in France, the following spring in England, and finally some months in Italy. The letters were written at the request of a Nürnberg physician, to whom they were addressed and who with the writer's consent had published some of them before they all appeared in book form.[6] They deal primarily with topics of special interest to the medical profession. The writer frankly bases his estimate of the different countries on the results of his investigations of the hospitals, the insane asylums, the sanitation, and the general state of medical practice.[7] He refers the reader to Archenholz and Wendeborn for more comprehensive views of England, observing, however, that the former is too lavish with his praise, while the latter is too prone to find fault. Schaeffer was a loyal German, with a pronounced antipathy against France and a strong predilection for England. He had studied at Strassburg, and, like Goethe, had

[6] *Briefe auf einer Reise durch Frankreich, England, Holland und Italien in den Jahren 1787 und 1788 geschrieben,* 2 vols., Regensburg, 1794.
[7] *ibid.,* Vol. I, p. 23.

only become the more German in this French environment.[8] Referring to France, he says:[9] "We Germans are certainly fools for wishing to pattern ourselves after such a frivolous nation and for currying favor with a people who at heart despise us and whom we far surpass in thoroughness, uprightness, kindness and sturdy character." Apparently Dr. Schaeffer had not formed a high opinion of the medical institutions of France. He found them, in fact, poorly equipped, badly managed and shockingly unsanitary. His description of the General Hospital in Lille is representative of his findings:[10] "On the outside this extensive building looks very well, but within everything is à la Françoise unclean and malodorous (*schmutzig, unrein, stinkend*)." In Italy the situation was but little better. In short, Schaeffer's ethnographical studies tend to prove the superiority of the Germanic races over their Latin neighbors.

After the hospitals it is the theaters[11] that attract our traveller most strongly. In this field the French make a better showing. "The costumes of both actors and actresses, as invariably in Paris, are magnificent, tasteful and appropriate to the occasion." The acting is good, "though it is said to have been incomparably better a few years ago." The one fault common to French actors is their exaggerated declamation.

In London Schaeffer and his party made the usual rounds, Covent Garden, Drury Lane, Saddler's Wells, Ranelagh, Vauxhall, Royal Circus, and in addition Royal Grove, as Astley's Riding School had been recently renamed. Astley was already known to the tourists from his frequent appearances in Germany. In the two leading theaters they saw "some of the best actors, such as King, Kemble, Parsons, Mrs. Crouch, Mrs. Siddons, etc."[12] Generally speaking, the trage-

[8] Schaeffer studied at Altdorf and Strassburg 1771-1774. Goethe left Strassburg in August 1771 and Schaeffer presumably did not arrive till later, hence the two were probably not fellow students.

[9] *Briefe*, Vol. I, p. 196.

[10] *ibid.*, Vol. II, p. 155.

[11] On French theaters, *Briefe*, Vol. I, pp. 66ff.

[12] *ibid.*, Vol. I, p. 297.

dies were "incomparably better than the comedies. In the latter the actors exaggerate their rôles and everything is turned into caricature." Mrs. Siddons was Mrs. Siddons. When she played the part of Mrs. Beverley in *The Gamester,* "everybody wept." Scenery and costumes were in the best of taste. The galleries were sometimes noisy, showing a rudeness unknown to "uns Teutschen," yet far exceeded by the Italian theater public.[13] Schaeffer appears to have attended the theater less in London than in Paris, owing perhaps to his deficiency in the English language. He tells us that Sir Joseph Banks and other scientists laboriously mustered all their French in order to converse with him, or patiently listened while he murdered the King's English.[14] However, he was not always compelled to speak a foreign tongue, for he found "eine unzählige Menge Teutscher" in London.[15] This friendly visitor attempts to correct a number of false impressions of the English then current in Germany. He had been led to believe that they were gloomy, morose, disagreeable, and, if not rude, at least indifferent towards foreigners. Just the opposite he found to be the case:[16] "Scholars as well as the common people are unusually polite to strangers, far more affable and more modest than the Parisians." Nor was the English nation so melancholy as the outside world fancied. On the contrary, they were only too fond of spectacles and distractions, and it seemed "that the majority of Londoners were just as incapable of serious pursuits as the Parisians and the Viennese."[17]

When the time came to leave "this favored land and its good inhabitants," Schaeffer was almost as distressed as was Sophie on the occasion of her departure. He embarked pronouncing a benediction: "May Heaven's richest blessing rest upon this beautiful, good country, and upon its happy and favored inhabitants, where a man is respected because he is

[13] *Briefe,* Vol. II, pp. 193, 250.
[14] *ibid.,* Vol. I, p. 220.
[15] *ibid.,* p. 240.
[16] *ibid.,* p. 219.
[17] *ibid.,* p. 295.

a man, and where one is esteemed and often rewarded not according to one's fortune, dignities and ancestry, but according to one's merits and integrity."

The number of southern Germans contributing to the *Reiseliteratur* on England increases as the century approaches its end. Günderode, Schaeffer and Sophie von la Roche are followed by Alexander von Wimpffen,[18] chamberlain to her Highness, the Duchess of Württemberg. Wimpffen spent a few weeks in England in 1788 or earlier. Concerning this visit he published what he terms "eine unbedeutende Schrift." He was in England again in 1793 for seven months, in 1795-1797 for nearly two years, and once more, from August 1799, to April 1800. However, his travel letters date mainly from his first visit. They were evidently based on the "unbedeutende Schrift" and supplemented with notes by the author. In this form they comprise the first two volumes of a work recording experiences and impressions of travel in many lands.[19] Wimpffen's pages bear the stamp of fairness, intelligence and erudition. His education had been French, and his earliest military service was in France. At times, in fact, he seems to look upon himself as a Frenchman and falls, accordingly, into the class of Germans branded by Schaeffer as fools. But these are only occasional lapses. At any rate he is well versed in classical and French literature, is familiar with the leading English writers, notably Thomson and Young, and even knows his Benjamin Franklin.

[18] On Wimpffen (born 1752) see *Biographisches Lexikon des Kaiserthums Oesterreich,* by Constant von Würzbach, Wien, 1888. Wimpffen was the son of Freiherr Stanislaus Gustav von Wimpffen and his wife, Julie von Latour-Foissac. He served as "royal French captain" in the German regiment La Mark and was advanced in the French service to the rank of general. He entered the service of the widowed Duchess of Württemberg in 1793 (?) as privy counsellor and chamberlain. At the time of his death he was a minister and Lord Steward of the King of Württemberg.

[19] *Briefe eines Reisenden geschrieben aus England und Frankreich, einem Theil von Afrika, und aus Nordamerika,* aus der französischen Handschrift übersetzt von P. J. Rehfues, Darmstadt, 1814.

Wimpffen is also the author of *Voyage à St. Domingue,* 1789; German version, Erfurt, 1798.

Wimpffen adds his voice to the chorus of protest against the German tendency to overrate everything that comes from foreign countries in general and from England in particular. Here he shows no inclination to masquerade as a Frenchman. "It is scarcely believable," he says,[20] writing as a matter of course in French, "but nevertheless true that our readiness, so to speak, to throw ourselves upon the necks of foreigners, is one reason for their poor opinion of us." For his part, Wimpffen will report with pleasure all the good he knows of the British, but when truth demands, he will, "though with pain, also mention the evil." Just what contacts he had with Englishmen does not appear. He was an intimate friend of Lord and Lady Melville, however, whom he visited at Wimbledon Common, and doubtless had a wide acquaintance in polite English society. He is sufficiently open-minded to give the English preference in certain respects over his beloved Frenchmen, and adds his bit towards convincing the German people, who should have abandoned the idea long since on the strength of evidence and arguments presented by German travellers, that the English were not gloomy, taciturn and unsociable, and inclined in foggy weather to shoot or hang themselves or one another. They were on the contrary quite cheerful on occasions and were even loquacious on the subjects of politics, love and war—ideas corresponding closely enough to the three words listed by Heine as the essentials of the German language: Brot, Kuss, Ehre. Among the "evils mentioned with pain" is the fact that "the British government acted arbitrarily, inconsistently, unjustly and injudiciously in the measures which it took first against the city of Boston and then against all the colonies."[21]

In things literary Wimpffen shows his French schooling, yet he is catholic enough in his tastes to admire Lessing as an exponent of enlightenment along with Voltaire. He is still protesting against *Sturm und Drang* tendencies at a time when they have pretty well run their course. He delivers to

[20] *Briefe,* Vol. I, p. 80.
[21] *ibid.,* p. 186.

Lady Melville a lecture on German letters to which he should have added footnotes after becoming acquainted with some of Goethe's and Schiller's mature works. He recognizes the fact that the Germans have made great progress in literature in the past three or four decades, but feels that they are still somewhat in the dark as to literary values. In berating them for their poor taste he does for once give them credit for a patriotic attitude:[22]

> If one believes them, no nation equals the Germans today in literature. Milton, Shakespeare, Corneille and Voltaire are easily outranked by Klopstock and their dramatic poets. Schiller speaks only with contempt of Corneille and Racine. He himself ruthlessly violates the rules which—I will not speak of Boileau—but which Aristotle, Quintilian, Longinus and Horace have prescribed, and yet is in the eyes of his nation the sublimest of all dramatic poets. . . . The common fault of German playwrights, and the last they will discard, since it is based on Shakespeare's example, which is for them the supreme authority, is the practice of introducing into one and the same play the low beside the noble and the trivial beside the sublime, adding to the Vatican Apollo a beard, and to the Medicean Venus the breasts of Alecto. Meanwhile a few clear heads are beginning to rise in protest against this presumptuousness and against the bad taste which, under the pretext of truthfulness to nature, violates all the principles of art with the more impunity since the German public, having had no opportunities for the cultivation of an æsthetic sense, applauds with enthusiasm the most grotesque and often the most immoral plays. But the lasting and deserved applause bestowed on the *Nathan* of the late Lessing and on a few of Iffland's and Kotzebue's comedies, as well as Collin's tragedies *Regulus* and *Oktavia,* proves that the German public only requires good models in order to learn to applaud what really merits approval.

One hardly hopes to find a partisan of the young Schiller among Württemberg courtiers, but there is no reason why

[22] *Briefe,* Vol. I, pp. 206-7.

Wimpffen should continue to judge the dramatist by *Die Räuber* when at least *Don Carlos* is at hand. And certainly Schiller's mature plays and his post-Kantian aesthetics, which had been published before Wimpffen's manuscript was put into final shape, should have found favor with his fellow Württemberger.

In the course of the century since Muralt wrote his *Lettres sur les Anglois* the London stage had apparently developed no new tradition in the treatment of foreign characters, but continued to make them appear as ridiculous as possible. Soon after his arrival in England Wimpffen saw a play[23] in which a French coxcomb, "who seemed to have the leading rôle," came off very badly. English dramatists had the less reason to represent French in such an unfavorable light, Wimpffen argues, since the French, when introducing an Englishman into a play, "almost always choose a man worthy of respect."[24] Such cultivation of "odious prejudices" was unworthy of a great nation:[25]

> Why have most dramatic poets this mania for seeking only among a neighboring people errors, absurdities and vices which are abundant enough at home? If comedy is to correct our faults by making us laugh at them, how can it fulfill its purpose whilst aiming all its arrows at foreign countries?

The theater ought to be "the true school of morals." At the same time, while Wimpffen will not go so far as to say with Voltaire that it is better that the morals of a people degenerate than their manners, he insists that English dramatists err in "following the taste of the common people rather than that of a certain class." The stage "should adhere to the tone of good society" and not descend to the level of the masses.

[23] A footnote, evidently by Rehfues, suggests that it was *König von Schlaraffenland*. Possibly this conjecture refers to Legrand's *Roi de Cocagne* (1718).

[24] This statement is fairly well confirmed by Harry Kurz in his *European Characters in French Drama of the Eighteenth Century*, New York, Columbia University Press, 1916; see pp. 203, 232*ff*.

[25] *Briefe*, Vol. I, p. 104.

"The Attic salt, of which the Athenians were so fond, would not be savory to the palate of the Drury Lane pit. The latter requires ocean salt and demands the sort of wit and humor which produces the ringing laughter known in that country as 'horse laugh' (!)." Fortunately there are Englishmen who have "cultivated their taste in the French school" and recognize that Shakespeare, "whose characters almost always have one foot on the cothurnus and the other in a wooden sandal," great as his genius may be, is nevertheless "far inferior to Corneille, Racine and Voltaire, if not as a poet, certainly as a dramatist."[26]—This division of Shakespeare into dramatist and poet would seem to be a symptom of the transition then under way from *Sturm und Drang* to Romanticism. To the former school Shakespeare was the greatest of all dramatists; to the latter, the poet par excellence.—As for comedy, the French were still further in the lead:[27] "The English theater has a few original poets who have composed a few original pieces in the comic genre, but they can not bear comparison even with the second rate French writers of comedy." A long list of plays by Destouches, Gresset, Piron, Beaumarchais and others is drawn up in substantiation of this claim. Nothing is said of Sheridan or Goldsmith. As for opera, Paris easily takes the lead over London.[28]

Once more we hear that the actresses are abler than the actors, this time because in England as elsewhere "women are generally better impersonators (*Komödianten*) than men." The males mistake carelessness for nature, and pompousness for nobility. The limit of clumsiness and poor taste is reached when an English actor plays the part of a French *petit-maître*. On his first trip to England Wimpffen found that the theater public was still quite unceremonious.[29] Late-

[26] *Briefe,* Vol. II, p. 196.
[27] *ibid.,* Vol. I, p. 108; cf. Vol. II, p. 198.
[28] Wimpffen's discussion of opera (Vol. II, pp. 113*ff.*) is of interest. He points out the fact that the Paris opera-goer desires not merely a vocal concert but a *mélodrame*. This perhaps accounts in part for the favorable reception of Gluck's operas in those days and of Wagner's later.
[29] *Briefe,* Vol. I, p. 108.

comers in the pit engaged freely in long-distance conversation with their acquaintances in the gallery. But on his subsequent visits he observed that "the London spectators were far quieter and better behaved" than formerly.

Jacques Henri Meister (1744-1826) was bound to France by quite as strong ties as Baron von Wimpffen. His father, a native of Zürich, was French court pastor at Bückeburg in Schaumburg-Lippe, and his mother was a French Huguenot. In 1747 the family removed to Erlangen and in 1757 returned to Zürich. Here young Meister was a favorite student of Bodmer at the Carolinum until 1766, when, to his mentor's dismay, he associated himself with the French *encyclopédistes*, especially Diderot and Grimm. His literary activity, which he began as the French translator of Gessner, covered a wide range—fiction, history, religion, philosophy, politics—and won for him a high position in the intellectual life of his day. Most of his works were written in French and in a style which puts to shame such desecrators of that tongue as Pöllnitz, Bielfeld and Reinhold Forster. He rated Racine above Shakespeare, but as a disciple of both Bodmer and the *encyclopédistes* he owed much to England, and he was broad enough in his culture to appreciate English literature highly in spite of his preference for French.

Meister spent a fortnight in London in 1789 and was in England again for six months in 1792. His travel impressions are recorded in the usual epistolary form. The first letter was published in Paris in 1791, others appeared in German translation in Archenholz' *Minerva,* and the whole collection as the work of a *dame émigrée* in Reichard's *Olla Podrida.* The complete French edition appeared anonymously in Zürich in 1795.[30] The author admired some aspects of English life as much as had Archenholz, whose *Tableau d'Angleterre* he cites. His first impression was one of amazement that "a country situated but a short distance from our continent presents such a totally different appearance in respect to the nature of the soil, the general atmosphere, architectural

[30] *Souvenirs de mes Voyages en Angleterre,* 2 vols., Zürich, 1795.

forms, customs, language, and social manners."[31] But on closer examination many of these differences were seen to be advantages. "Such an atmosphere of cleanliness, prosperity and security" was entirely new to this visitor. Besides, the food was quite to his liking, "du bon befsteak, des patatos, du royal plum-pudding et de l'excellent fromage de Chester(!)" And Englishwomen were more beautiful than Frenchwomen; and still more beautiful in 1792 than in 1789, better dressed and better *coiffées.* The explanation for this improvement is probably that Meister's first visit was in the summer, when London was less adorned by feminine beauty than in other seasons. As for the political system, it elicits as strong praise from this visitor as it had seventy-five years earlier from his Zürich fellow townsman Haller:[32]

> It seems to me that I had not taken fifty steps on British soil before I sensed a spirit of liberty that I had never experienced up to that time, not even on the day when with other heroes, curious like me, I had the honor of being among the first to tread in triumph upon the ruins of the Bastille.

Of the British constitution he says:

> I see nothing comparable with it either in ancient or in modern history. It is in my opinion the masterpiece of political contrivances. There is no other, it seems to me, by which the different powers composing and maintaining the social order are divided and recombined in a fashion so well calculated to give at the same time sufficient efficiency to the supreme power and sufficient energy to personal liberty.

Yet the theatrical censorship, entrusted solely to the Lord Chamberlain, who was responsible only to the King, seemed to him inconsistent with British principles of freedom.[33]

According to his own statement, it was the theater that Meister studied perhaps "with the greatest care" during his

[31] *Souvenirs,* Vol. I, p. 2.
[32] *ibid.,* pp. 39*ff.*
[33] *ibid.,* p. 33.

second and longer residence in England.[34] On his first visit,
despite his poor command of the English language, he found
that he was able with text in hand to understand all of the
twelve to fifteen plays he saw (in the course of two weeks!)
except those too local in their appeal for the comprehension
of a foreigner, such as Foote's *The Minor*. He was surprised
to find that one-half of these plays were translations from the
French. This was due of course to the first enthusiastic reaction in London to the events of the French Revolution.
Meister saw *La Prise de la Bastille* admirably presented in
three different theaters, Astley's (Royal Grove), Royal Circus
and Saddler's Wells.[35] On his second visit he evidently had
the language better in hand.

Meister appraises the relative merits of French and English drama with his usual perspicacity and fairness.[36] While
missing "the noble simplicity, the purity, the elegance and
the delicacy" of Corneille and Racine in English poets, he
admires the latter for their vigor and variety and the broad
sweep of their imagination, and recognizes the supreme
genius of Shakespeare, as poet if not as artist, the more
readily "since M. de Voltaire himself is convinced of it,"
M. de Voltaire, whose plays are themselves "models of perfection." Regarding the English claim for the supremacy of
their own theater over all others, and speaking for the moment as a Frenchman, he says:

> It is a superiority that France will doubtless never recog-
> nize. But is she entitled to act as judge in her own cause?
> If the case were brought before the tribunal of the differ-
> ent European nations, there is every reason to suppose
> that we should lose it in Spain and Germany. We might
> take comfort, however, in the thought of winning it in
> Italy and especially in ancient Greece.

[34] For Meister's discussion of the theaters see Vol. II, pp. 61-94. References are given below only to passages not included in this section.

[35] *Souvenirs*, Vol. I, p. 53; Professor Nicoll (*op. cit.*, p. 54) mentions
the first two of these productions.

[36] *Souvenirs*, Vol. I, pp. 93-105.

In Meister's opinion French translations of Shakespeare were calculated to do untold harm, "turning our young people from the study of the only models that may be imitated with impunity."

English comedy is also found wanting when weighed in the balance against French. As tragedy appeals to Englishmen only by means of "very forceful and very varied situations," comedy satisfies them only through the presentation of "very complicated plots, very positive characters, very lively, original repartee"; hence they have "a comedy bordering more or less on caricature." And "the indecency, the extreme immorality of the majority of their comedies" is difficult to reconcile with the usually high moral standards of the English people. Meister knows of no theatrical work in which there is *"plus de verve et d'esprit,"* for example, than *The Beggar's Opera,* but at the same time he can think of none more immoral and more dangerous.

The first English tragedy which Meister saw in London was *Romeo and Juliet.* Miss Esten, whose youth, beauty, and expressive, sonorous voice afforded ample compensation for any deficiencies in her acting, was appearing for the first time in the "touching rôle of Juliet." Meister thought the play "just as monstrous as all the other masterpieces of its author, but resplendent with the same beauties." Yet, though cognizant of the "monstrosities" therein, he had no patience with the practice of altering Shakespeare's texts. Some of them, he lamented, had been disguised beyond recognition, such as *The Tempest* in Dryden's version. Likewise in *Macbeth,* in which Mrs. Siddons and Mr. Kemble were giving a splendid performance, there was too much that was not Shakespeare, too much bad taste and shabbiness in the costumes of the witches, and all in all too much claptrap. He found it insufferable that Banquo should take the part of his own ghost and felt that the audience should behold the specter only in Macbeth's terror, as was the case with the banquet guests. "Mr. Kemble has desired on several occasions to suppress the ghost," Meister says, "but has never had the courage to do so." Another source of regret was that "the prodigious admiration which Shakespeare's tragedies had inspired had almost caused his comedies to be forgotten." But, like Wendeborn before him, Meister observed that with all the veneration for Shakespeare the tragedian, the theater public was more responsive to the works of lesser lights. At any rate he saw with his own eyes that *Jane Shore, Venice preserv'd, The Grecian Daughter* and *The Gamester* drew more tears than the works of the master.

Meister seems to have been one of the first to stress a need which the Shakespeare theater at Stratford was eventually to fulfil:

> There is not a hall in London large enough for the mountings which the production of English tragedies requires. Of all modern theaters it is assuredly the English that can least dispense with a vast deep stage, since I know of none on which the scenery is more often changed and on which there are more situations demanding pomp and circumstance. Why has not national pride conceived the idea of erecting a handsome monument to the glory of dramatic art, an edifice where the adored masterpieces may be presented with due magnificence and splendor? It is not indifference to the delights which this enchanting art affords, for I believe that spectacles have never been more popular in France and Italy than at present in London.

Certain peculiarities of the English stage strike the foreign eye and ear. The popular actor must bow, no matter what the situation, upon first appearing on the stage; an actor passes invariably to the right as his interlocutor passes to the left, and vice versa; the affected prolongation of certain cries and exclamations; the sort of "organ-point" by which all the oh's and ah's are emphasized; the frequent transports in which the actors feel compelled to precipitate themselves full length to the floor, and the frightful noise of these oft-repeated plunges. Furthermore, the diction seems at first exaggerated, violent, harsh; but this is the true spirit of the language, and one becomes accustomed to it. Regardless of such faults, and although he knew the London stage at a time when it could claim fewer really great actors than usual, Meister formed a high opinion of English acting. On his first visit he was unable to see Mrs. Siddons, but he "repeatedly saw with great interest" Mrs. Kemble, Mrs. Brooke and Mrs. Bannister. His special favorite among them was Mrs. Kemble, who reminded him of Mlle. Doligny and was "naturalness and sensibility personified." But it was the rare talent of Edwin that impressed him most. There was "in the play of his features, in the tone of his voice" an irresistible comic force. With the finesse of a Préville and the realism of a Raffanelli, the greatest comic actors Meister had seen hitherto, Edwin combined a more genuine and natural gaiety, strange though it seemed that "the merriest comedian of the day was neither in France nor in Italy, but beneath London's cloudy sky." But the stage was soon to lose this gifted actor. His worthiest successor, Meister found on his second visit to England, was the younger Bannister, who lacked Edwin's spontaneity, directness and frankness, but was possessed of more grace, subtlety and sprightliness, and besides had "very lively eyes and the most beautiful teeth in the world." In Otway's version of *Les Fourberies de Scapin* "his make-up and acting left little to be desired," even in the opinion of a spectator who had seen both Préville and Feuli in the same rôle; and as the little apothecary in *The Prize,* a musical farce by P. Hoare, "one of the prettiest little pieces given this winter," Bannister equalled Dugazon in caricature and at the same time remained true to the spirit of the part and played it with the greatest verve and comicalness imaginable. Meister likewise admired King, Lewis and Kemble, but did not care for Sweet, and could never reconcile himself to the "strange grimaces" of Dodd, who played "our beaux, our young marquis, our *petits-maîtres,* our Fleuris and Molés." Like Wimpffen he saw no reason why Frenchmen should always be represented as ridiculous creatures.

In writing of Mrs. Siddons and her acting Meister becomes as eloquent as Ernst Brandes. He brings her to life in a vivid

pen-portrait and represents her as probably the greatest
actress of all times. He pronounced her at any rate the greatest he had ever seen, but in fairness added that he had seen
only the *"derniers débris"* of Mlle. Dumenil, and had known
Mlle. Clairon only in society, "where indeed she was charming beyond compare." Mrs. Siddons had succeeded a score of
times in making him forget that he was listening to a foreign
tongue, he who had formerly laboriously followed English
plays with text in hand. He was unaware that it was actually
Mrs. Siddons whom he saw before him, it seemed rather to
be in turn Lady Macbeth, Calista, Belvidera, Jane Shore,
Volumnia. Never for a moment did she lose her innate charm
and dignity of bearing, "not even in the convulsive laugh preceding the death of Isabella" in *The fatal Marriage.* "Tears,
sobs, terror, despair, the most abject horror, far from dis-
figuring her noble features, only render them the more expressive and the more interesting." Her only equal in tragedy
on the London stage was her brother, Mr. Kemble, and he
only in certain rôles, such as Macbeth, Shylock, Coriolanus.
While he rated Kemble higher than did most critics, Meister
found besides him no men who could equal the Frenchmen
Saint Prix and Vanhove; and the women, excepting Mrs.
Siddons, were "scarcely more distinguished." He admires
Miss Esten for her youth and beauty, as he had three years
earlier, "but her talent is even more youthful than her appearance, and will perhaps always remain so." Miss Pope has
seen her best days. Miss Powel is well endowed with nobility
and sensitivity, but her speech is too slow, too sad, too
monotonous. In comedy there are several actresses of rare
ability, especially the fascinating Miss Farren, and Mrs. Jordan. Miss Farren is particularly charming in *The School for
Scandal* and Burgoyne's *The Heiress,* the two modern English
comedies which Meister likes best. These two plays seem to
him, in fact, to "present the most faithful and vivid picture
of present-day manners" and at the same time to have "all
the wit, all the vitality of ancient comedy, at least as much
of both as is compatible with the decency of the characters,

the general interest of the action, the plausibility of the dialogue, and elegance of style." Mrs. Jordan was less versatile than Miss Farren, but "her charm was more simple, more naïve, and the gaiety of her acting fresher and more contagious." Among her best rôles were Hypolite in Cibber's *She Wou'd and She Wou'd not* and Miss Peggy in Garrick's *The Country Girl,* an adaptation of Wycherley's *The Country Wife.*

Accustomed to hearing Mandini, Viganoni and Morichelli, Meister was not easily captivated by the London singers, but he was of the opinion that the English were improving perceptibly in musical taste, their operas being musically on a much higher plane than they were "only three or four years ago." Pretty Mrs. Storace and the celebrated Mme. Mara (Elisabeth Schmeling) were still sure of applause, and lovely Mrs. Crouch, though a pronounced English type, had nevertheless "a voice worthy of Naples or Rome." Miss Bland and Miss Decamp were very good, though their singing was marked by *"le goût du terroir britannique."* Among the male vocalists Incledon, Dignum and Kelly were outstanding.

This visitor had no fault to find with the behavior of the late-century theater audience. He was not the man to take offense at occasional manifestations of the spirit of liberty. He did note the frequent demands in those days of nationalistic exaltation for "God save the King," and was highly entertained by a little scene he witnessed at Saddler's Wells. As usual there had been calls in accents *"très peu mélodieux"* for music, music, and then an insistent demand for "God save the King."—"Annoyed doubtless by these oft-repeated cries, someone with a very piercing voice put a stop to them all by shouting in a humorous but impatient tone which provoked a general laugh, 'God save the King, God save us all!' "

George[37] Forster (1754-1794), the son of Reinhold For-

[37] The younger Forster bore the English name George. So far as I have found, Ina Seidel is the only modern writer to mention him without Germanizing his name.

ster, saw England rather through native than foreign eyes.
Hence perhaps the discrepancies and contradictions in his
views. A cosmopolite by nature and circumstances, he was
more at home in England than anywhere else. His love for
that country, though strong, did not blind him to its imperfections, and he was Englishman enough to love it the more
for some of its faults. He was so imbued with the English
spirit, in short, that he was unable to view England objec-
tively, or even with an objectivity modified by some more or
less definite personal bias, as did many of those whose opinions we have heard. With George Forster the situation is
more complicated, and it is this complication rather than
instability or lack of a point of view[38] that accounts for his
apparent wavering. His notes on England, though fragmentary, bring out effectively many of the lights and shadows
of the English scene and compose a little volume which for
its aesthetic merits stands alone in all the eighteenth-century
German literature of travel treating of Great Britain.[39]
George Forster had many contacts with Germans sojourning
in England. Bahrdt, Moritz, Archenholz, Wendeborn and
Raspe are among those known to have been associated with
the Forsters, father and son. On his return to Germany the
younger Forster was cordially received at Göttingen, especially by Lichtenberg and by his future father-in-law, Heyne,
who was also the brother-in-law of another distinguished
Englandfahrer, Ernst Brandes. He likewise belonged at one
time to Sophie von la Roche's circle. When returning to
England in 1790, after an absence of twelve years, he carried
with him a letter from Sophie to Warren Hastings. On this
journey he was accompanied by Alexander von Humboldt,
then a young man of twenty-one.

[38] As Elsasser seems to think; *Politische Bildungsreisen,* pp. 96f.
[39] *Ansichten vom Niederrhein, von Brabant, Flandern, Holland, England und Frankreich im Frühjahr 1790,* Vol. III on England, in Reclams Universalbibliothek. References below are to *Briefe und Tagebücher Georg Forsters von seiner Reise am Niederrhein, in England und Frankreich im Frühjahr 1790,* hrsg. von A. Leitzmann, Halle, 1893.

As an ardent democrat who was to become fatally embroiled in the French Revolution, George Forster admired England first of all as the home of political freedom. While he felt that tradition counted for too much and reason for too little in shaping the English political system, he nevertheless found that liberty, equality and fraternity prevailed in England to a far greater degree than in other European countries. "Nobility is discernible here in culture and character down to the very lowest classes," he declared. Social distinctions were less marked than on the Continent. There was "intimate intercourse among people of all ranks," and the humblest man was treated at the inns as well as the greatest lord.

Although Forster had promised to write for his friend Huber[40] a full report on the London theaters, he was unable to do the subject justice, for his visit was in the summer. His first letter from England is dated May 23. Mrs. Siddons had departed before his arrival, "and with her the finest tragedies of the season were gone."[41] He had already written Therese, his wife, a review of Frederic Reynold's *The Crusade*.[42] Of the other new plays, he failed to see Cobb's *The haunted Tower,* which was said to be musically pleasing but devoid of common sense. *No Song, no Supper,* a musical farce which he saw, was "of the same sort, but is redeemed to some extent by the voice and acting of Mrs. Storace, an Italian singer who has learned English thoroughly. The very pretty music is composed by her husband, stolen from Pleyel, Grétry and Giordani." Reynold's *The Dramatist,* a self-portrait, is "full of wit and allusions to local customs, but without dialogue." In fact, "no attention is paid any more to good dialogue; effect is all that is demanded. One goes to the theater to see, scarcely any longer to hear." This state of affairs suggests

[40] Member of the Körner-Schiller-Stock group in Leipzig. Ina Seidel's interesting historical novel *Das Labyrinth* gives an authentic account of George Forster's checkered life.
[41] *Briefe und Tagebücher,* pp. 114*ff.*
[42] The letter is apparently not preserved.

to Forster that "the Kotzebues, if given a dose of salts, would make their fortune here too," as they actually did a few years later. Of the older pieces Forster mentions but two, *The Rivals* and *The Beaux' Stratagem*. On both he makes some interesting comments. *The Rivals* is "a great comedy, sparkling with wit, has well drawn characters, and also dialogue. . . . The suspicious lover, Faulkland, is admirably drawn, and his Julia has a femininity that is now rare on the English stage." Miss Farren played the rôle of Julia quite well, but in high comedy she cannot approach Mrs. Abington, who at last has retired. Miss Farren is given more admiration than she deserves, "a fault which all theater audiences in all countries have in common at present." Here Forster passes over to generalities. Tragic diction is highly perfected on the English stage, being "very precise, very pure and distinct," but in the case of Kemble, the leading tragedian, too monotonous. "Garrick and his school," with whom, of course, Forster was well acquainted. "had more real emotional fire or were better able to simulate it." The actors now read their lines too coldly, with too much studied emphasis. Yet Kemble is quite talented, and his innate dignity is the more impressive since his delivery is measured, unless the situation calls for rapid speech. "While his declamation is not song, it is more than ordinary discourse." Stately demeanor is characteristic not only of Kemble, but of English actors in general. The explanation is to be found, Forster thinks, in the social conditions under which they live:

This dignity, this decorum, this *gentleman-like air* in the rôles of kings and heroes I have never seen on the German stage, because there the actor on such occasions is not *natural* enough, or, like Koch, is *too* natural. In a word, the *feeling* of a great man is lacking; and I am inclined to believe that their familiar association with people of all classes . . . gives the actors here a certain natural nobility.

A revival of "that splendid comedy" *The Beaux' Stratagem*
gave Forster a good opportunity to compare the actors of
1790 with those of an earlier and more glorious period :[43]

> Mr. Lewis as Archer, Mr. Quick as Scrub, and Mrs.
> Pope, the former Miss Younge, as Mrs. Sullen[44] gave
> me a very feeble impression indeed of Garrick, Weston
> and Mrs. Barry in these same rôles. Mr. Lewis was not
> at all what he is supposed to be, a gentleman disguised
> as a servant, but was a servant assuming the manners
> of a gentleman. Scrub is supposed to be a stupid, igno-
> rant rustic into whose brain an idea penetrates now and
> then. But Quick played the part so that he seemed to
> divine and guess too much. Weston was well aware that
> this character was not to be entirely lacking in native
> wit, but he represented him as devoid of actually ac-
> quired ideas, of trained mental powers, and this is the
> proper way to play the part. And Mrs. Pope, an actress
> whom I find quite pleasing, has neither liveliness nor
> humor enough for the rôle of Mrs. Sullen. She plays it
> with dignity, but without comic effect.

The farce *Love in a Camp*,[45] which was given after *The
Beaux' Stratagem,* is dismissed as "insufferably banal and
wretched."

In Birmingham on their last theater evening Forster and
Humboldt saw *The Country Girl* and Lloyd's *The Romp*,[46]
"not the most brilliant plays of the English theater." But
a certain Mrs. Davis, of Manchester, gave a remarkable ex-
hibition of physical prowess and acrobatic skill. She was con-
tinually "leaping and hopping about." As for the other actors,
Forster adds in one of his slightly enigmatic phrases, "suffice it to say in their praise that for the first time since I left
Germany I was vividly reminded of certain German troupes."

George Forster is the ablest dramatic critic among our
travellers excepting Lichtenberg and Sturz and perhaps Bran-

[43] *Briefe und Tagebücher,* p. 218.
[44] In the German text, Mrs. Smallen.
[45] *Patrick in Prussia; or, Love in a Camp,* by John O'Keefe.
[46] *Briefe und Tagebücher,* p. 254.

des. No remarkable critical acumen of any sort can be claimed for Friedrich Wilhelm von Hassell, who is next in the procession. He is notable only for his expansive benevolence and chronic optimism. A captain in the Hanoverian infantry, he was called to England in 1790 as tutor to an English prince,[47] and thus saw something of the life in court circles. He became acquainted with Burke, Reynolds and West, visited in company with the Duke of Gloucester the notorious Chevalier d'Éon, and attended, as had Forster and Humboldt, a session of the Warren Hastings trial, which was "the sublimest scene" he had ever witnessed. Like Forster, too, he was deeply impressed by one of the Händel festivals, "such a spectacle as only London could offer." Enthusiastic over the Shakespeare Gallery, Vauxhall, Ranelagh and practically everything else he had seen, Hassell quit England after a sojourn of ten months, pronouncing a benediction upon the land similar to the blessing already invoked by Schaeffer: "Pleasant, happy isle, farewell! Thou standest at a height of culture and felicity that makes me dizzy. Thy chief enemy is thine own greatness. May Providence preserve thee! Since I have become better acquainted with thee, thy destiny is of great concern to me!" The benevolent captain had no literary aspirations, but, undaunted as he professed to be by the fact that so much had already been written about England, he resolved to record his impressions for the benefit of his family and accordingly addressed to his wife travel letters of sufficient volume to compose a book of two hundred and twenty-five pages, though of rather thin content.[48]

From the beginning of his residence in London Hassell worked away at the English language. He had probably not advanced sufficiently by the second day to understand the

[47] Evidently the son of the Duke of Gloucester; H. states (*Briefe aus England*, p. 48) that Reynolds is "now (Dec. 1790) engaged in painting a life-sized portrait of my prince in the academic costume of Cambridge, where the latter studied, as a gift to the university." William Frederick, only son of William Henry, first Duke of Gloucester and Edinburgh, was born January 15, 1776, and received the degree of M.A. at Cambridge in 1790. Reynolds had previously painted him in 1780.

[48] *Briefe aus England*, Hannover, 1792.

performance he attended at Drury Lane. At any rate he tells us nothing of the play itself, but says:[49] "It was in every respect a beautiful spectacle—acting, singing, orchestra, scenery, the magnificent illumination, the crowded house, the perfect quiet broken only by applause, which to be sure was thunderous." A few weeks later[50] he was able to understand something of Sheridan's *Critic* at the same theater. He was not favorably impressed. In fact, for the first time he uses strong language to express his disapproval. The whole play was "exaggerated even to the extent of the most ghastly caricature."—"Starke Speise muss man dem englischen Publikum vorsetzen," he observes. Yet the acting at times came up to the high standard which he found usually maintained in England. The next play mentioned is *The School for Scandal,* which this spectator had seen "quite as well performed several times" in Hanover. But at last he saw Mrs. Siddons and gained "an entirely new conception of the stage."[51] He confesses his inability to describe her acting, "which alone is worth a trip to England, for it is certainly unique." But upon seeing her in *Jane Shore* and *The Grecian Daughter* he could not refrain from the attempt.[52] "I have seen Mrs. Siddons again, and how!" he exclaims in one of his frequent transports. "Oh, if I were only a dramaturgist like Knigge,[53] so that I might describe what I saw!" Even without this advantage he does very well. Rowe's play was not altogether to his liking, but it was at least an excellent vehicle for Mrs. Siddons' art, which he reviews in detail. Two scenes were unforgettable. Jane's timid approach to the home of a friend whom she had robbed of her lover: "She staggers up to the door, timidly lifts the knocker, releases it as if she had committed a mortal sin, seizes it a second time and—knocks. It is impossible to describe how she knocked, but I shall never forget

[49] *Briefe aus England,* p. 18.
[50] December 4.
[51] *Briefe aus England,* p. 52.
[52] ibid., pp. 92-100.
[53] Adolf Franz Friedrich Ludwig Freiherr von Knigge "gab 1788f. *Dramaturgische Blätter* heraus." A.D.B.

her in this situation, never forget the tone of her voice in
answer to the servant, never the timidity, the anguish of her
expression and movements." And her reunion with her husband. Thinking it is his ghost, she starts back terrified. After
portraying the whole scale of emotions, horror at the supposed apparition, then, on recognizing her husband, abject
fear, humility, penitence, then hope of pardon, and finally
the realization that she is forgiven, "she seizes his hand in
silence, presses it to her lips and kisses it fervently three or
four times." During this entire pantomime she bore in the
eyes of her German admirer a striking resemblance to Frau
von Hassell. "The poet certainly never thought of this hand-
kissing, yet it was certainly a most effective touch." Finally,
at the conclusion of the scene, she died quite realistically in
her husband's arms. "Perhaps a certain paleness still clung
to her from her recent illness," Hassell continues, "but certain it is, one could actually see her die and rejoiced with her
when she said at the end, 'Now all is well, and I shall sleep
in peace.' " It did not occur to this spectator, as it had to
Alberti, that *Jane Shore* was an immoral play, and it is probable that the young clergyman would not have considered it
so, if he could have based his opinion on Mrs. Siddons' interpretation of the leading rôle. Like Sophie von la Roche the
Hanoverian soldier seemed to consider tears the best evidence
of great acting, and Mrs. Siddons, "without saying a word,
could draw tears from all eyes." In *The Grecian Daughter,*
when called upon to save her father's life by murdering his
enemy, she performs the awful act "with such dignity, not
to say grace, that one loves the hand by which the deed was
done. It is rather an anxious thrust of the dagger for the
father's protection than a murder, and the unfamiliar weapon
glides at the very same moment from her trembling fingers.
But when she actually saw the enemy lying dead at her feet
and her father standing in safety before her, what emotions
followed one another in her features! . . . Finally her knees
bent involuntarily in holy prayer, and the very arm which had
just committed murder was stretched gently towards heaven,

as if to say, 'Forgive me, Judge, thou knowest I had to do it.' "[54] This touching pantomime lasted fully five minutes, and the entire audience was as deeply moved as the tender-hearted German visitor; "on all sides nothing was to be heard save sobbing and soft applause."

One of the many pieces current at the time in London representing scenes from the French Revolution, *Tableau de Paris,* given at Drury Lane, is also described. Everything was caricature—the Assemblée Nationale, in which the president's voice could never be heard above the din; ruffians everywhere in evidence, the lamp-post, Lafayette, Mirabeau, barbers with drawn swords, and ladies with little push-carts.—The presence of the King and Queen with six princesses of the blood added to the glamour of the occasion, and the lusty singing of "God save Great George our King" was most stirring.

The new theater in the Haymarket, which had just been completed, impressed Hassell with its beauty and magnificence. He enjoyed there "the ballet *Orpheus and Eurydice,* with Tartarus and Elysium." Vestris, the dancer, and David, the singer, carried off the honors.

In Friedrich Wilhelm von Schütz[55] we might naturally expect to find a competent theater critic, since he was a specialist in that field. He had begun in his student days at Leipzig as a reviewer of current plays,[56] and was subsequently editor of a *Theaterzeitung* in Hamburg.[57] He is more concerned with the drama and especially with character analysis than with acting. It may be that he derived from the plays he saw in London some new standards of measurement for future use as a critic, but his contribution to the German discussion of English theaters is slight. His brief visit to London was towards the close of the same season in which Mrs. Siddons

---

[54] This line sounds somewhat more reverent in Hassell's German: "Vergieb mir, Richter, ich musste es ja thun!"

[55] Born 1758; date of death unknown.

[56] *Dramaturgischer Briefwechsel über das Leipziger Theater im Sommer 1779,* Frankfurt und Leipzig, 1780.

[57] See Hill, Wilhelm, *op. cit.,* pp. 118f.

had swept Hassell off his feet,[58] but he apparently did not see the great actress, for he does not mention her name.

By the last decade of the century German tourists felt constrained to apologize for adding to the volume of travel literature on England. Hassell, for instance, wrote for the future delectation of his family. Schütz takes up his pen in order especially to retouch Archenholz' *Tableau d'Angleterre,* bringing out more of the shadows essential to a true picture. He feels impelled to offer an antidote to the anglomania only slowly subsiding in Germany. He accuses not only Archenholz but also Moritz, Lehzen and Wendeborn of partiality to England, but for some strange reason exempts Büschel, who is actually more guilty of the offense than any of the others. Schütz is determined for his part to make his own observations and to paint things as they are. His intentions are undoubtedly honest, but in his laudable desire to do justice to his fatherland he detracts from the glory of England as had none of his predecessors with the single exception of the disagreeable Professor Büsch. Schütz admits that he "observed much good in London and saw much beauty"; but he found far less of both than he had been led to expect. He subscribes to the view that "the English constitution is a masterpiece," but he declares that "the vaunted freedom" is largely imaginary, as the disillusioned foreigner discovers at the outset through the strictness of the customs officials.[59] The Händel festival at Westminster Abbey was most impressive, and the German prima donna Mme. Mara was a great artist, though her voice had far more volume in her Berlin days.[60] There was much to be said in favor of the Quakers.[61] But St. James's Park was not to be compared with the Berlin Tiergarten; and "any one accustomed to German

[58] *Briefe über London, ein Gegenstück zu des Herrn Archenholz' England und Italien,* Hamburg, 1792. Although Schütz gives no exact dates in his letters, the time of his visit is fixed approximately by the fact that he saw at the Pantheon the opera *Idalide,* of which the première was on April 30, 1791; see Nicoll, A., *op. cit.,* p. 356.

[59] *Briefe über London,* p. 5.

[60] *ibid.,* pp. 39, 130.

[61] *ibid.,* pp. 263f.

coffee-houses is not likely to find much pleasure in those of England."[62] The "fat Englishmen" were not precisely things of beauty,[63] and their dress was somewhat bizarre in the season of 1791. Their Saxon cousin was amazed to see them parading in St. James's Park in "flesh colored trousers with stockings to match." Furthermore he found it difficult to distinguish between mistress and maid in England,[64] just as Küttner had in his theater stall, and likewise the Frenchified Bellarmine who graces the pages of *Joseph Andrews*. They all complained that there was not sufficient distinction between the two classes either in dress or in coiffure. And as for English freedom, if the customs officials had left any illusions on that score, a single Sunday in London ought to suffice to remove them; "a foreigner afflicted with British liberty fever could certainly find no better day for being cured."[65]

Schütz was not precisely the man to interpret the culture of one great nation to another, yet somebody, so he claimed, had asked him to write an account of the London stage. This was certainly one of the subjects on which German visitors to England and their friends most desired enlightenment. Boie had charged Lichtenberg to make a study of the theaters for his *Deutsches Museum,* and Huber had made a similar request of George Forster. Schütz has at least the merit of treating the subject systematically[66] and, in accordance with his resolutions, of forming his own opinions. In the first place, the houses themselves were not so spacious as one would expect to find them in a city as large as London: "Drury Lane, in comparison with German theaters, was only of medium size."[67] A unique feature of the English stage was the afterpiece, in which the greatest variety of entertainment was offered, and for which the seats, hitherto comparatively empty, were invariably filled to capacity; for after the first acts of

[62] *Briefe über London,* pp. 56, 80.
[63] *ibid.,* pp. 74, 86.
[64] *ibid.,* p. 91.
[65] *ibid.,* p. 116.
[66] *ibid.,* pp. 30-45.
[67] Schütz evidently overlooked the recently rebuilt Haymarket.

the main play, the price of admission was reduced by half. As
for the acting, "Germany could point to men quite equal to
English players." In fact, the greatest tragic actors whom this
visitor saw in London seemed to him but *Haupt- und Staats-
aktionenschauspieler* in comparison with their contemporaries
on the German stage. Schröder, whose art was in perfect
harmony with nature, could put to shame the whole school
of English actors, who violated all of the classic rules which
Hamlet had laid down for their profession.[68] Serious faults
were noticeable also in the comic acting. Here the critic rests
his case on one shocking example:

> The chambermaid in making her exit passed the burning
> candle under the lackey's nose, so that the light was ex-
> tinguished. I am sure that the director of a good German
> theater would punish such insolence. But in Drury Lane
> general applause betokened approval. The natural conse-
> quence was that the actress in question sought to exag-
> gerate her playing even more in the next act, whirled
> around on one leg for joy over a new dress and threw
> herself to the floor in a position not in keeping with fe-
> male propriety.

To avoid the appearance of "an exaggerated partiality to
German actors," Schütz notes some good points of the English. They memorize their parts thoroughly and seem independent of the prompters. The latter are behind the scenes, so
that the spectator's illusion is not marred by a souffleur's box
in plain view on the stage. "Furthermore," he continues, "the
decorations of the English theater are magnificent, and the
painted scenery is excellent. In this respect it completely surpasses all German stages." The same is true of music and
lighting, "for in both cases economy is not carried so far as
in Germany, since both are considered essential to a well

---

[68] There is every reason to suppose that no actor (and but one actress)
on the London stage from Garrick's retirement to the end of the century
was the equal of Schröder. But English actors in general probably appeared to Schütz and other foreign visitors to be overacting, at least
partly on account of the fact that they heard them in a more or less unfamiliar language.

equipped theater." As for the stage machinery, it is not all that might be expected in royal theaters. In England, as in Germany, for instance, trees are planted on the stage before the eyes of the spectator, without any regard for his illusion. If he had lived long enough to see the first performance of Tieck's *Der gestiefelte Kater* in 1844, Schütz would doubtless have been horrified.

The Italian opera in the Pantheon elicits the highest praise from this critic, presumably because it is not English. "The house was filled, mainly with foreigners," he observes with evident satisfaction. The voices were excellent and the orchestra was bigger and better than any Schütz could remember having heard in a German opera-house. "The scenery, painted by William Hodges, was in both conception and execution worthy of such an excellent opera." After *Idalide* there was a charming ballet, *Le Siège de Cythère*. The popular places of amusement—Saddler's Wells, Ranelagh, Vauxhall—proved to be less disappointing to this visitor than Drury Lane and Covent Garden. Vauxhall in particular was found to be worthy of a visit from every foreigner. It was, in fact, unique, far surpassing "both in nature and in art" its many German imitations.

The deportment of London audiences, which, according to all reports, was steadily improving, was still at times far from perfect. Schütz seems to have witnessed some painful relapses. We hear nothing from him of the *schöne Stille* which made such an impression on Friedrich von Hassell. On the contrary:

The uproar before the play begins is indescribable. . . . Not only orange-peels but sometimes even glasses of water or other liquids are thrown from the gallery into pit and boxes, so that frequently spectators are wounded and their clothing is soiled. In short, such outrages are committed in the name of freedom that one forgets one is in a playhouse which claims in its advertisements the title of Royal Theatre. In Germany such disorder would never be tolerated even at a marionette theater in a village inn. At Drury Lane I wished to look around at the gallery in order to examine its structure, but a heap of orange-peels, striking me with considerable force in the face, robbed me of all curiosity. The best plan is to keep your face turned towards the stage and thus quietly submit to the hail of oranges on your back. On one occasion my hat was so saturated (I really do not know with what watery ingredients) that I was compelled to have it cleaned next day at the hatter's.

His neighbors, he adds complacently, fared no better. And a lady, whose own hat was repeatedly dislocated, assured him "that the audience had been on its best behavior today." When the music began, to be sure, the house quieted down at once. But it seemed ready to explode again on the slightest provocation.

With all their flair for English failings Büsch and Schütz cannot compete with Andreas Riem (1749-1807), who writes ten hundred and fifty pages for the express purpose of proving to the world that the British are the scum of the earth.[69] From 1795 on Riem resided in Paris. Whatever the motive behind his malicious attack on England, his miserable screed is unworthy of serious consideration. Its worthlessness was recognized at once,[70] promptly gaining for it the oblivion it deserved.[71] The highest praise for anything English from this source is silence, and such praise is bestowed on the London stage. However, there is an occasional favorable comment on some aspect of English life, made for the obvious purpose, under the semblance of fairness, of adding weight to the almost exclusively destructive criticism. Typical of the author's drift is his one and only comment on the theater:[72]

[69] *Reisen durch Frankreich, England und Holland in verschiedener, besonders politischer Hinsicht.* In den Jahren 1785 und 1795, von dem Canonicus Riem, auf Kosten des Verfassers. 8 vols., Leipzig, 1795-1801. Vols. IV and V on England.
[70] See, for example, Wimpffen, *op. cit.,* Vorrede, for Rehfues' opinion.
[71] The work is rare. The Preussische Staatsbibliothek possesses only Vol. I. The Bayerische Staatsbibliothek and the Breslau Universitäts-bibliothek have complete sets.
[72] *Reisen,* Vol. V, p. 326.

I attended a performance of Shakespeare's *Othello* at Drury Lane. The English have their own peculiar style of acting and producing plays. Mrs. Siddons gave a masterly performance in the rôle of Desdemona. The bandit rôle of Iago was played well, and in truly British fashion. The actor committed murder with cold, calm cruelty bordering on indifference. In Germany or France the actor would have shown in the murder scene the satisfaction of knowing his wrongs revenged, and an emotional conflict. Not so the Britisher. He played the rôle of Hastings, Clive and the British agents in India.

Nothing more could be desired from this source, unless it were the report of an attack from the gallery.

An increasingly unsympathetic attitude towards England is evident in many quarters in Germany during the closing years of the century, reaching the pitch of positive hostility among the more ardent partisans of the French Revolution. There were also those who discredited England in a deliberate attempt to cure their fellow countrymen of the anglomania about which so much is heard during the last third of the century. Schleiermacher, according to his own statement, took this stand.[73] But Andreas Riem's rabidity is without parallel.

Theodor von Schön (1773-1856), the noted Prussian statesman, spent as a young man a year of travel and study in England which bore fruit for the rest of his life. "Durch England wurde ich erst ein Staatsmann," he said towards the end of a long and distinguished career. As a student at Königsberg he had been introduced by Professor Kraus to English political theory and particularly to Adam Smith's school of thought. In order to prepare himself further for his sojourn in England, he turned quite naturally to Göttingen. Archenholz, Wendeborn and Küttner were his guides on his trip to England, and his friend Weiss was his travelling companion. After a few weeks in London in the spring of 1798 the two young men made a tour of England and Scotland, returning in October to the capital, where they remained through the

[73] Schleiermacher, F., *On Religion,* "Speeches to its Cultivated Despisers," translated by J. Oman, London, 1893, pp. 9-10, 23.

winter. Schön kept a diary after the manner of Uffenbach and Kielmannsegge, filling his pages mainly with the daily routine, illuminated only now and then by personal observations and deductions. When he does offer an interpretation of the facts compiled, it is with telling insight and comprehension. This diary, however, like one or two other works we have taken up, loses some of its interest through its long deferred publication and consequent lack of influence on the German mind. Here again is such an observer as George Forster, with an eye for both the strength and the weakness of English life. The nation is inhospitable and self-centered, we hear once more, after having been all but convinced of the contrary, and the upper classes are sadly lacking in genuine culture. The chief national virtues are integrity and above everything else patriotism, a quality which the future statesman longs to see emulated in Germany.[74]

Schön was an eager theater-goer, not only in London, but wherever he happened to be—Edinburgh, Newcastle, Liverpool, Manchester, Birmingham, Weymouth. A new chapter in theatrical history, Kotzebue in England, claimed his attention.[75] His first impression of the London stage was derived from a matinée at Covent Garden,[76] where "a satirical piece treating of the French plan for an attack" was given. Patriotism was the keynote of the occasion. The criticism of the performance is laconic: "The actors played well." On the same evening Schön tried to gain admission to Drury Lane, where Kotzebue's *The Stranger*[77] was to be played, but the house was filled before his arrival. He saw the play, however, three days later and found that it had been well translated, but that "the Stranger was represented rather as a savage than as a misanthrope." German visitors were generally shocked by the liberties which translators and producers took with

[74] *Studienreise eines jungen Staatsmanns in England am Schlusse des vorigen Jahrhunderts,* Berlin, 1891, pp. 35, 138, 155, 203, 240.
[75] On this subject see Thompson, L. F., *Kotzebue, A Survey of his Progress in France and England,* Paris, 1918.
[76] April 16, 1798.
[77] Benjamin Thompson's translation of *Menschenhass und Reue.*

Kotzebue's plays in adapting them to the English stage. The "dose of salts" which George Forster had prescribed was sometimes given too generously. In this instance the producer catered to English taste by inserting a peasants' dance to celebrate the arrival of the lord. At the beginning of the third act, furthermore, the Stranger's servant calls upon two young girls for songs, an addition to the original text which the translator evidently realized was out of place, for he has the Stranger say, "What is this for? I wish to hear no music," whereupon the servant offers his apologies, adding, "If you don't care for it, then let it be for my sake."[78] In general, we are informed, the London performance retained but little of the spirit of the play, but at any rate, "the audience was pleased and wept mightily." This was the twelfth performance, and the house was packed. Soon after the opening of the following season Schön saw a second Kotzebue play,[79] *Lovers' Vows,* Mrs. Inchbald's translation of *Das Kind der Liebe.* The English version was still less satisfactory than in the case of *The Stranger.* Evidently the play was too good for Mrs. Inchbald, our German friend suggests, "for she felt compelled to ruin it. Some of the best lines and finest thoughts are entirely omitted. . . . The play is decidedly the weaker for the changes in the characters of the Count and the Baron. According to the author's purpose, the one represents the ideal of a simple, open character, and the other that of a fop. The latter is in this instance half fop and half a refined gentleman. . . . But the worst feature is the costumes. The landlord and the servants are dressed in the German style of Charlemagne's time, and all the others in Hungarian attire, including the Count, who is certainly anything but an officer." *The Stranger* was at this time still drawing large houses. Schön saw it again and thought that Kemble gave a better interpretation of the title-rôle than he had the previous season and that "Mrs. Siddons played the part of Eulalia quite well," but that the costumes were still rather odd. Another

[78] This interpolation does not appear in the printed text of *The Stranger.*
[79] Covent Garden, October 29, 1798.

German play which Schön saw was *Adelaide and Abelard*(?),[80] "a very ordinary product of the German muse."

In the course of a year in England Schön managed to see seven Shakespeare plays. He does not indulge in criticism of the dramas. The debate on Shakespeare, with the authority of Lessing for the defense and that of Voltaire on both sides, is a thing of the past, having ended, so far as our travellers are concerned, with Wimpffen. Schön saw *Romeo and Juliet* in Edinburgh (July 23). Mrs. Pope, whom he frequently refers to as his "favorite," was Juliet, and her husband was Romeo. Though he had often seen this play in Germany, he had never seen the two leading parts so well acted. Mrs. Pope reached at times such heights, in fact, that he was inclined to consider her the greatest actress he had ever seen. His enthusiasm was such that he went to see her again in the same rôle two weeks later in Manchester. His admiration was only increased. Her gentle dignity and convincing sincerity in portraying the heroine's emotions was in Schön's opinion nothing short of perfection. In Manchester he also saw *Cymbeline* (Aug. 29). Miss Robertson read her lines badly—"Shakespeare's marvelous thoughts lost much in being spoken without any expression." After his return to London he saw Kemble as *Richard III* (Nov. 29) and considered his acting great only at rare intervals. He also saw "a new actor" give a very poor performance as Macbeth at Covent Garden.[81] Later he saw *Measure for Measure* and *Much Ado about Nothing* well played, and finally a performance of *Hamlet* with Kemble in the title-rôle, which was on the whole admirable. The German spectator was amazed, however, that the audience showed so little interest in this masterpiece.

Schön held no very high opinion of other English drama-

[80] Schön saw this play at Covent Garden on December 12, 1798. According to Genest (Vol. VII, p. 431), a play entitled *Albert and Adelaide* was performed in that theater on December 22, 1798, for the ninth time; he says of it: "This heroic Romance is said in the bill to be taken from the German—not printed."

[81] The new actor was Turner. Schön saw "his first appearance on any stage," December 15, 1798; see Genest, *English Stage,* Vol. VIII, p. 431.

tists. Like the majority of foreign visitors, he soon discovered that English tragedy was superior to English comedy, both as literature and in the performance. He accredits himself as a critic by pronouncing *The School for Scandal* and *The Rivals* the best modern English comedies of those he saw.[82] Two plays by Thomas Moore, *A Cure for the Heartache* and *The Way to get Married,* rather appealed to him.[83] The former was "a very comic comedy," and the latter "was not so bad as English comedies usually are," and was the more enjoyable on account of Mr. Quick's excellent acting. Cumberland's *The Jew* was the best of a number of plays seen in Weymouth,[84] and the elder Colman's *The jealous Wife* was "one of the best English comedies."[85] Murphy's *The Apprentice* seemed worth seeing a second time, being "one of the English farces which, with all its crudities, contains a good deal of wholesome wit,"[86] and was improved by Bannister's able acting. The operetta *Inkle and Yarico,* by George Colman, the younger, based on an old story which Gellert had treated,[87] was most enjoyable. Here again Quick's acting was delightful. This was one of several plays of that season which protested against the slave trade. The people showed plainly their disapproval of the traffic in human beings, yet it continued unabated.[88] Beaumont and Fletcher's *Rule a Wife and Have a Wife*[89] was characterized by "mediocre wit and little sense." Mrs. Inchbald's *Everyone has his Fault* was "not extraordinary," but was redeemed by Mrs. Pope's stirring acting;[90] and the same author's *The Wedding Day* and *The Child of Nature* were worth while only on account of Mrs.

---

[82] *Studienreise,* p. 204.
[83] *ibid.,* pp. 138, 152.
[84] *ibid.,* p. 157.
[85] *ibid.,* p. 200.
[86] *ibid.,* pp. 204, 212.
[87] Gellert's *Sämtliche Fabeln und Erzählungen,* Volks-Ausgabe, Leipzig, 1880, Book I, p. 13.
[88] *Studienreise,* p. 153.
[89] Drury Lane, February 4, 1799.
[90] *Studienreise,* p. 117.

Jordan's art.[91] Mrs. Inchbald's *Animal Magnetism*[92] Schön
seems to have mistaken for a translation from the German.
The Castle Spectre, by Monk Lewis, which the two travellers
saw in Edinburgh, Liverpool and London, was "quite sense-
less."[93] *Die schöne Kriegslist*[94] and Hoare's *My Grandmother*
were worth seeing on account of Quick's acting again. Reynold's *Laugh when you can* was only mediocre,[95] and even
Mrs. Pope was a disappointment in it, while Cobb's *Ramah
Droog* was positively dull.[96] And *The Beggar's Opera,* in
spite of its threescore years and ten, was still shocking to
foreign ears.

Aside from the condemnation of Gay's masterpiece, the
modern critic would doubtless concur on the whole in these
contemporary opinions of the English theater at the end of
the century. But Schön found full compensation in Mrs. Siddons' acting. It was after he had seen the divine Sarah in
several rôles that his "favorite," Mrs. Pope, began to shrink
in his eyes. He saw the greatest of English actresses first in
The Gamester.[97] She was Mrs. Beverley, and her brother was
Beverley. Both were excellent, for "in such extravagant scenes
the English are masters." Soon afterwards he saw her in
The Grecian Daughter.[98] This time he observes that "the English perform such plays well, better in fact than other nations;
but they are quite incapable of drama"—which is to say,
probably, that they excel in tragedy but not in high comedy.
But the most memorable of this theater-goer's evenings was
when he saw *Isabella* with Mrs. Siddons in the title-rôle. He
saw this play three times.[99] The first time he thought that "Mr.
Kemble and Mrs. Siddons played extraordinarily well," that
this was in fact the best performance he had seen. The second

[91] *Studienreise,* p. 210.
[92] Weymouth, September 22, 1798.
[93] *Studienreise,* pp. 123, 188.
[94] *The Belle's Stratagem* (?).
[95] *Studienreise,* p. 198.
[96] *ibid.,* p. 190.
[97] Drury Lane, November 6.
[98] Drury Lane, November 16.
[99] Drury Lane, December 3 and December 16, and March 26, 1799.

time he was convinced that Isabella was Mrs. Siddons' best rôle; and finally, of his last theater-evening in London, he writes: "This evening I was at Drury Lane and saw the great actress, Mrs. Siddons, for the last time, in the rôle of Isabella. She displayed all her powers, and I left the magnificent house almost convinced that I shall never see a tragic rôle better played." These reserved climactic comments on Mrs. Siddons' acting attest to Schön's innate ability as a dramatic critic.

An anonymous work, *Sittengemälde von London,* gives a picture of the English stage at the close of the century. The author was presumably Peter Will, pastor of the German Church in the Savoy.[100] While he appears to bestow praise rather reluctantly, he does find some occasion for favorable comment. For instance, "such cleanliness prevails as can be

[100] There is some uncertainty as to the authorship. In the catalog of the Preussische Staatsbibliothek it is stated that the author is Johann Christian Hüttner. Meusel's *Das gelehrte Teutschland* (Vol. XXI) lists this work as follows: "Will (Peter), *Sittengemälde von London,* hrsg. von H., Gotha, 1801." In the same source (Vol. VIII) we read: "Will, Peter, Prediger einer teutschen Gemeinde zu London, geb. zu Darmstadt. Unter dem Namen Peter Teuthold gab er heraus: *The Necromancer, or the Tale of the Black Forest,* founded on facts, translated from the German of Laurence Flammberg, 2 vols., London, 1794." Possibly Hüttner was the "H." who edited Will's *Sittengemälde.* The author states that he has been living in London for more than ten years. J. G. Burkhard (*Kirchengeschichte der deutschen Gemeinden in London,* Tübingen, 1798), lists Peter Will among clergymen connected, from 1790 on, with the German Church in the Savoy. Holzmann & Bohatta attribute a work of precisely the same title (giving the date of publication as 1802) to Carl Ludwig Fernow, Weimar librarian. This is a mistake, for Fernow was apparently never in England. He did publish an account of his travels in Italy, in part as a corrective to Archenholz' unfavorable picture of that country (*Römische Studien,* 3 vols., 1803-1806). Further evidence that Will and not Hüttner is the author of the work in question is that the latter would have shown more admiration for England. Carl Gottlieb Horstig, who visited in London in 1803 his "Freund und Landsmann" Hüttner whom he had known thirty years earlier in Guben, says of him (*Reise nach Frankreich, England und Holland,* p. 210): He "is now living in his own home in London and maintains that a foreigner who has lived five years in England will be satisfied in no other country, owing to the indescribable charm of England." Hüttner's writings on England are far more complimentary than the *Sittengemälde von London. Das gelehrte Teutschland* is very probably right in assigning it to Will.

found nowhere else in Europe, not even in Holland";[101] and "the English language may be set to music just as well as any in the world, and is in the highest degree singable, as Händel and a number of English composers, notably Purcell, have proved."[102] But unfortunately "certain ladies and gentlemen in authority" maintain that Italian is the only musical language in the world and that only Italian singers are worthy of attention from the true connoisseur. Consequently "Italian nonsense" alone is offered in the opera, while such masterpieces as Händel's *Artaxerxes,* Purcell's *Comus,* and Arne's *Alexander's Feast* are entirely neglected. Likewise Italian singers are always sure of a sympathetic hearing, while "a Billington must seek abroad the applause and support which her own country owes her, but ungratefully withholds." At the same time the English are more passionately fond of music than any other Europeans, not excepting the Italians and the French, and the arrival of a famous violinist or pianist produces a greater sensation in fashionable circles than the conquest of a hostile island. It seems, from the foreign point of view, that art was cultivated in England largely as a fashionable pursuit even before the Victorian age. Our chronicler continues:[103]

> People of high and low estate are so music-mad that their daughters must above all things learn to play the piano or the harp or some other instrument, whether they have musical talent or not. . . . One pays a Clementi a guinea for an hour of instruction, while one pays scarcely a fourth as much for a lesson in the German language, although it is now the fashion to learn German.

But with all their devotion to art, the Londoners have very little musical appreciation. Theatrical taste is equally poor. In fact, "there was perhaps never a time when the London stage had so few good actors and actresses as in our days, and when theatrical taste had sunk so low."[104] We have completed a

101 *Sittengemälde,* p. 23.
102 *ibid.,* p. 50.
103 *ibid.,* p. 53.
104 *ibid.,* p. 56.

circle in our investigation and arrived again at the starting point; for this critic finds the same faults in the London theaters as Muralt had a century earlier. Everything is adapted to the taste of the rabble rather than to standards of dramatic art; and talents, if there be any, prostitute themselves in order to win the plaudits of the mob. The situation was quite different in Garrick's day. The actors of the old school sought to educate the public. But now :[105]

> Mrs. Siddons is the only player in either of the two theaters of whom the tragic muse has a right to be proud. Her brother, Kemble, is admired as a star of the first magnitude. But, though possessed of really great talent, physical comeliness and a rich, well modulated voice, he is totally lacking in refined taste and correct judgment. His speech and gestures are affected in the extreme, and when he aims at deeply stirring effects, he howls so that the spectator is reminded of Virgil's *ululatus magnorum luporum*.

Kemble would be one of the greatest actors in Europe, had he not allowed himself to be spoiled by the depraved taste of his public. Likewise Cooke, though hailed as a "tragic *Wunderkind*," will, for want of sound criticism, never achieve real greatness. The same is true of Munden, Fawcet, Quick and Johnston.[106]

As evidence of the poor taste of the London public, the reception accorded to German plays is cited :[107]

> You will scarcely believe it, but unfortunately it is only too true that Lessing's masterpiece, *Emilia Galotti,* was hissed here, that Iffland's *Jäger* was rejected by the theater directors as a stupid piece, and that an excellent translation of *Götz von Berlichingen*[108] did not repay the

[105] *Sittengemälde,* p. 58.
[106] *ibid.,* p. 64.
[107] *ibid.,* pp. 59f.
[108] There were by this time three English translations of *Götz*—those of Rose D'Aguilar (1795), Rose Lawrence (1799), and Walter Scott (1799) ; see Morgan, B. Q., *Bibliography of German Literature in English Translations,* Madison, 1922, pp. 167-8. Perhaps the superfluity of translations accounts in part for the poor sales.

publisher for the paper on which it was printed. *Wallensteins Tod,* the masterpiece of our German Shakespeare, would perhaps have been favorably received despite the corrupt taste of the London public; but Coleridge, the translator, has so marred the beauties of the original that it can never be produced in its present form. Unfortunately this clumsy translation has given the great man such an evil name here . . . that his *Maria Stuart,* which has been admirably translated,[109] has not yet succeeded in finding a publisher. It will probably appear in the *German Museum,* and then justice may be done to this finished drama. . . . Schiller's *Räuber* has been unusually well received by the reading public, but the King's Chamberlain, who is responsible for the censorship of new plays . . . , can not be induced to give his permission for its performance, for the noble spirit of liberty permeating it is incompatible with the principles of freedom which actuate our governments since the beginning of the French Revolution.

A further indication of lowered standards is seen in the enthusiastic applause bestowed upon Sheridan's *Pizarro,*[110] "a piece without plan or character, a veritable monstrosity with the head of a lion and the body of a monkey."[111] With all their imperfections, this critic adds, Kotzebue's serious dramas might have been expected to improve the public taste, in view of their superiority over anything of the kind produced in recent years in England, but *Menschenhass und Reue, Kind der Liebe,* and other Kotzebue plays were anglicized in such a fashion that whatever aesthetic values they possessed in the original were lost.[112] As for comedy, the situation was still worse:[113] "Our new comedies are for the most part nothing but caricatures and would be hissed off the German stage."

Through the first years of the nineteenth century Germans continued as much as ever to visit England and to write of

109 Charles James Mellish was the translator.
110 An adaptation of Kotzebue's *Rollas Tod.*
111 *Sittengemälde,* p. 61.
112 *ibid.,* p. 62.
113 *ibid.,* p. 63.

their impressions, but the increasing distress brought upon their country by the Napoleonic wars was soon to reduce this activity, and it is safe to say that it never again loomed so large in German life and thought as it had during the last quarter of the old century and at the beginning of the new. Later on Heine, Grillparzer, Friedrich von Raumer, Pückler-Muskau, Fontane and others wrote interesting accounts of their travels in England, but the heyday of *Reisebeschreibungen* was past. By 1803 in addition to Hüttner, who has already been mentioned, Esther Bernard, Joachim Heinrich Campe, Johann Friedrich von der Decken, Christian August Gottlieb Goede, a Leipzig jurist, Joseph Salamo Frank, a distinguished Viennese physician, and Karl Gottlob Horstig, inventor of one of the earliest stenographic systems, had visited England and written on the whole readable accounts of their travels.[114] The "sentimental journey" has gradually evolved into a typical product of Romanticism, which is the order of the day from Horstig to Pückler-Muskau.[115] With the exception of Frank, who confines himself to scientific matters, all these writers discuss the theater, most of them at

[114] Bernard, *Briefe während meines Aufenthalts in England und Portugal an einen Freund,* Hamburg, 1802; pp. 100-20 on English theaters.

Campe, *Neue Sammlungen merkwürdiger Reisebeschreibungen für die Jugend,* 6 vols., Frankfurt und Leipzig, 1806; Vol. V, pp. 51-70 on English theaters.

Decken, *Versuch über den englischen Nationalcharakter,* Hannover, 1802; pp. 135ff. on theaters.

Goede, *England, Wales, Irland und Schottland,* Erinnerungen an Natur und Kunst aus einer Reise in den Jahren 1802 und 1803, 5 vols., 2nd ed., Dresden, 1806; Vol. III, pp. 180-288 on theaters.

Frank, *Reise nach Paris, London und einem grossen Theile des übrigen Englands und Schottlands in Beziehung auf Spitäler, Versorgungshäuser, übrige Armen-Institute, Medizinische Lehranstalten, und Gefängnisse,* 2 vols., 2nd ed., Wien, 1806; does not discuss theaters.

Horstig, *Reise nach Frankreich, England und Holland zu Anfange des Jahres 1803,* Berlin, 1806; pp. 164ff. on English theaters.

[115] Horstig's opening lines afford sufficient evidence: "In stille Dämmerung verhüllen sich die Strassen der Stadt. Wohltätige Ruhe breitet sich allmählig über das Herz aus; und aus den Wellen der Weser, die wir nach wenig Stunden erreichen, trinken wir Vergessenheit der unruhigen Sorgen, die unsere Abreise erschwerten. Der Mond leuchtete zu unsrer neuen Fahrt. . . ."

considerable length. They pay high tribute to Mrs. Siddons and to Kemble and Cooke, but otherwise find the London theaters seldom superior and frequently inferior to those with which they are acquainted on the Continent. It is apparent enough that the English stage, though graced by the greatest actress of all times, was on the whole below its usual standard, while the German stage, thanks mainly to the much maligned Gottsched, to Lessing, to the influence of English drama and the English theater, and to the great contributions of Goethe and Schiller, was on the upward grade.

The soberer tone which marks German discussions of English theaters towards the end of the eighteenth century is traceable not only to the decline of the London stage both as to repertoire and performances, but also to an altered point of view, to a new orientation. Roughly speaking, we may say that a pronounced anglomania held sway in Germany from the Seven Years' War to the French Revolution, coloring the German reaction to everything English. It might be claimed that the wave of sympathy with the revolutionary cause which swept over Germany, though it soon subsided, broke once for all the spell of anglomania. In the first half of this period the German attitude towards England was determined largely by the rationalistic trend, in the second half by the tendency of *Sturm und Drang* towards the popular and emotional. Both currents were to a considerable extent derived from England, and the representatives of both felt drawn towards the main source of their ideology, the one group through their reason, the other through their emotions. That the *Stürmer und Dränger* entertained certain misconceptions as to England, for which a prose translation of Shakespeare was to no slight degree responsible,[116] is beside the point. Their admiration for England was all the greater for being based largely on feeling and intuition. As each of these sets of ideas in turn lost its hold on the German mind or came to be taken for granted, anglomania in Germany declined. There are of

[116] See Gundolf, F., *Shakespeare und der deutsche Geist*, VIII. Auflage, Berlin, 1927, p. 186.

course men of many minds in every country and in every age. Such distinctions as we are here drawing are naturally only relative. Such extremists as Andreas Riem prove little or nothing. It might be said, for instance, that Hassell's enthusiasm and Schaeffer's tender leave-taking of England smack of the *Sturm und Drang,* and so they do; but these men do not strike the dominant note of their generation.

Synchronizing fairly closely with the cooling off in Germany towards the English stage, there is under way a definite revival of respect for the French tragedy. Goethe and Schiller and others less than they, having repented of their *Sturm und Drang* excesses, draw gradually nearer both in their critical views and in their creative works to Corneille, Racine and Voltaire. Schiller, it is true, continues to write disparagingly of the French dramatists, but his mature plays belie only too plainly his theoretical repudiation of Voltaire's type of tragedy.[117] From now on French literature will on the whole be looked upon more favorably in Germany. Lessing had been inclined to spare only Molière and Diderot, and the *Stürmer und Dränger* only Rousseau in their general condemnation of French writers. As the result of such propaganda, the German public had been blinded for more than a generation to the merits of French literature. It is at least an interesting coincidence that the English stage lost ground with German spectators somewhat in proportion as English literature ceased to eclipse French literature in Germany.

In the closing years of the century German writers continued to stress the Englishman's relish for theatrical performances and the rapt attention with which he was wont to follow them. The praise of staging, scenery, lighting, incidental music, and usually of costumes is unstinted. In fact, Christlob Mylius is the only German visitor in the whole course of the century who has serious fault to find with such aspects of the London stage. At last the travellers have made up their minds as to the relative merits of tragic and comic

117 See Korff, H. A., *Voltaire im literarischen Deutschland des XVIII. Jahrhunderts,* 2 vols., Heidelberg, 1918, Vol. II, pp. 678*ff.,* 707*ff.*

performances to be seen in London. In the early years of the
century their preference was for the comedy, but finally, after
long wavering, they concluded that the real forte of the English was tragedy and that they surpassed in the tragic genre
all other nations.

As we have followed these fifty Germans on their visits to
English theaters, we have been able to trace a marked change
in their attitude and reactions, for which the gradual development of Germany into a great cultural nation is largely accountable. In the beginning they were almost entirely lacking
in critical discernment and taste. They then passed in turn
through the schools of Gottsched, Lessing and Herder and
ultimately emerged capable of forming opinions and estimates of their own. When Lessing had once supplanted
Gottsched as the arbiter of German drama, an anglomania
of varying degrees of intensity and of differing component
elements marked for three decades the German reaction to
the London stage and to everything English, finally to yield
to a more critical and frequently definitely unsympathetic
attitude.

BIBLIOGRAPHICAL APPENDIX

THE following list of German visitors to England in the eighteenth century, mentioned (with one or two exceptions) neither in text nor footnotes in the present study, is presented in the belief that it may be useful to future investigators of English-German cultural relations. This list is, of course, far from complete. Many other names of weight in various fields of German culture, notably in music, might be added. The works marked with an asterisk have been consulted as possible sources of material for the present study, but yielded nothing of importance.

*Bonstetten, Karl Viktor von (1745-1832), *Briefe von Bonstetten an Matthisson,* hrsg. von H. H. Füssli, Zürich, 1827. Bonstetten was in England 1769-1770. The earliest letters in this collection were written in 1795.

*Burkhardt, Johann Gottlieb, *Bemerkungen auf einer Reise von Leipzig bis London an eine Freundin,* Leipzig, 1763.

*Cordes, Ferdinand; a frequent contributor to *Deutsches Museum; Schreiben aus London,* May 5, 1786, *D.M.,* September 1786, pp. 281*ff.*

*Deichsel, Johann Gottlieb, *Reise durch Deutschland nach Holland und England, in den Jahren 1717-19,* Part III, "Aufenthalt in England," Bernouillis Archiv, Vol. VIII.

Fischer, C. E., *Medicinische und chirurgische Bemerkungen über London und die englische Heilkunde überhaupt,* Göttingen, 1796.

*Gentz (1764-1832), *Briefe von und an Friedrich von Gentz,* hrsg. von C. Wittichen, München und Berlin, 1910; Letters from London, addressed to Adam Müller, 1802; Vol. II, pp. 391-405.

*Hardenberg, Karl August Fürst von (1750-1822), *Denkwürdigkeiten des Staatskanzlers Fürsten von Hardenberg bis zum Jahre 1806,* von Leopold von Ranke, Leipzig, 1877. "Ein zweites kleineres Tagebuch liegt vor, in welchem Hardenberg die Reise beschreibt, die er über Holland nach England unternahm. Er hat sie am 31. Juli 1773 angestellt und ist erst am Anfang des folgenden Jahrs nach Hannover zurückgekommen." (Vol. I, p. 37.)

Jacobi, Friedrich Heinrich (1743-1819). "Im Jahre 1786 besuchte er in London den ihm befreundeten Grafen von Reventlow, welcher dort als Gesandter lebte." *A.D.B.*

Jerusalem, Johann Friedrich Wilhelm (1709-1789) ; cousin of Justus Möser and father of Karl Wilhelm Jerusalem (Werther) ; in England 1737-1740.

Kaufmann, Angelika (1741-1807) ; resided in London 1766-1781.

Körner, Christian Gottfried (1756-1831) ; friend of Schiller and of Archenholz; father of Theodor Körner; travelled 1779-1780 with Graf Karl von Schönburg in Holland, England, France and Switzerland.

*Nemnich, Philipp Andreas (1764-1822), *Beschreibung einer im Sommer 1799 von Hamburg nach und durch England geschehenen Reise,* Tübingen, 1800. Nemnich revisited England in 1805.

*Niebuhr (1776-1831), *Barthold Georg Niebuhrs Briefe an einen jungen Philologen,* hrsg. von C. G. Jacob, Leipzig, 1839. Niebuhr visited England and Scotland 1798-1799. See also *Die Briefe Barthold Georg Niebuhrs,* hrsg. von D. Gerhard und W. Norvin; Vol. I, Berlin, 1926, contains letters from England.

*Oeder, Johann Ludwig, *Beyträge zur Oekonomie-, Kameral- und Polizeywissenschaft aus den Berichten eines deutschen Kameralisten von seinen Reisen nach der Schweiz, Frankreich, Holland und England im Jahre 1759 und 1763,* Dessau, 1782.

Reich, P. Erasmus (1717-1787) : "the most famous publisher of his day." "Ueber seinen Aufenthalt in England und Schweden ist nichts bekannt." *A.D.B.*

Reichardt, Johann Friedrich (1752-1814) ; musician, author; visited London in 1785 and again in 1791.

*Taube, F. W. von (1728-1778), *Abschilderung der engländischen Manufacturen, Handlung, Schiffahrt und Colo-*

nien, 2. Ausg., Wien, 1777. Taube was born in London, where
his father, Christian Ernst von Taube, resided as physician to
Queen Charlotte.

*Titius, Dr. C. V., *Reisejournal von seiner im Jahre 1777
durch Deutschland nach Holland, England und Frankreich
angestellten Reise.* In *Bernouillis kurze Reisebeschreibungen,*
Vols. IX-XI.

*Vincke, Friedrich Ludwig Wilhelm Philipp von (1774-
1844), *Leben des Ober-Präsidenten Freiherrn von Vincke,*
nach seinen Tagebüchern bearbeitet von E. von Bodel-
schwingh, Berlin, 1853. Vincke visited England in 1800 and
in 1807.

Zimmermann, Eberhard August Wilhelm von (1743-
1815), scientist; travelled in the countries of northern and
western Europe 1767-1770.

INDEX

Abel, 76

Abington, Mrs., 48, 49, 53, 65, 76, 78, 79, 113, 121, 141

Adamberger, Mrs., 113

Addison, 32
> *Cato,* 15, 22, 76, 122

Aiken, 65, 86

Albert and Adelaide, 155 (80)

Alberti, G. W., 14, 21-3, 33, 83

Allgemeine Deutsche Bibliothek, 77, 93

Apelbald, J., 23

Archenholz, J. W. von, 50-6, 64, 72, 84, 92, 93, 98, 131, 139, 147

Aristotle, 18

Arne, Mrs., 78

Arne, T. A.
> *Alexander's Feast,* 159

Arnim, Bettina von, 59, 114

Astley's Riding School; *see* Royal Grove

Audiences, 26, 27, 31-2, 33, 54-5, 57, 62, 66, 72, 82, 86, 91, 97, 101, 113, 117, 118, 121-2, 125, 129-30, 131, 138, 150-1, 164

Bach, 76

Bahrdt, K., 73-5, 139

Baker, T.
> *Tunbridge Walks; or, The Yeoman of Kent,* 11 (10)

Banks, Sir Joseph, 76, 77, 125

Bannister, 100, 106

Bannister, Mrs., 136

Bannister, The Younger, 136

Barberina, Mlle., 20

Barelli, 50

Barry, 22, 25, 53, 78

Barry, Mrs. (later Mrs. Crawford), 49, 50, 113, 142

Bates, Henry
> *The Rival Candidates,* 48

Beaumarchais
> *Barbier de Séville,* 104

> *Le mariage de Figaro,* 104

Beaumont and Fletcher, 14
> *The Chances,* 12 (17)
> *Rule a Wife and have a Wife,* 29, 46, 156

Bedlam, 91, 117

Bellamy, Mrs., 55

Bernard, Esther, 162

Betz, G., 41 (38)

Bickerstaffe
> *The Padlock,* 40
> *The Sultan,* 113 (84)

Bielfeld, J. F. von, 4, 19-21, 23, 33

Billington, Mrs., 159

Bland, Miss, 138

Bode, 92

Bodmer and Breitinger, 24, 32, 41

Boie, H. C., 43, 63, 102, 148

Boileau, 7, 128

Boyce, Dr., 26

Brandes, E., 102-13, 139

Brandes, G. F., 102

Brandt, 27

Bretschneider, H. G. von, 57-8

Brockmann, 45 (38), 111

Brooke, Mrs. Frances, 136
> *Julie Mandeville,* 38
> *Rosina,* 97

Bruce, H. L.
> *Voltaire on the English Stage,* 20 (38)

Brückner, 96

Burgoyne
> *The Heiress,* 137
> *The Maid of the Oaks,* 48, 49

Burke, Edmund, 103, 143

Burkhard, J. G.
> *Kirchengeschichte der deutschen Gemeinden in London,* 158 (100)

Burnet, Bishop, 22

Burney, Miss Fanny, 66, 115, 116

Büsch, J. G., 71-3, 76, 80, 84, 147

Büschel, J. G. B., 89-91, 147

174   INDEX

Hagedorn, 15, 19, 21
Haller, 14, 15, 16, 24, 33, 63, 132
Hamann, 83-4
Händel, 14, 17, 20, 21, 65, 143, 147
   Artaxerxes, 159
Hartig, F. P. Graf von, 4, 66-71, 81
Hassell, F. W. von, 143-7, 150, 164
Hastings, Warren, 117, 139, 143
Haymarket, 11, 12, 13, 14, 23, 28, 50, 57, 78, 87, 91, 99, 116, 122, 146, 148 (67)
Heidegger, 20
Heine, Heinrich, 42, 52, 58, 127, 162
Henderson, 53, 76, 110, 111
Herder, 39, 44, 109 (76), 165
Heyne, 63, 102, 139
Hill, W.
   Die deutschen Theaterschriften des 18. Jahrhunderts, 24 (54)
Hoadly, B.
   The suspicious Husband, 22, 26, 42
Hoare, P.
   My Grandmother, 157
   The Prize, 136
Hodges, W., 150
Hogarth, 43, 44, 46, 47
   Analysis of Beauty, 24
Holberg, 24
Holland, 30
Home, John
   Douglas, 112
Hopkins, Mrs., 65
Horstig, C. G., 158 (100), 162 (115)
Howe, Sir William, 28
Humboldt, A. von, 139, 143
Hüttner, 93 (34), 158 (100)

Idalide, 150
Iffland, 123, 128
   Die Jäger, 160
Inchbald, Mrs.
   Animal Magnetism, 157
   The Child of Nature, 156
   Everyone has his Faults, 156
   Lover's Vows, 154
   Such Things are, 121

   The Wedding Day, 156

Jacobi, J. G., 44 (34), 114
Jagemann, 51
Jefferson, 65
Johnson, Samuel, 39
Johnston, 160
Johnstone
   The disbanded Officer, 116, 122
Jonson, Ben, 7
   The Alchemist, 29, 42, 46
   Everyman in his Humour, 29
   The silent Woman, 12
   Volpone, 25
Jordan, Mrs., 137, 138, 157

Kaufmann, Angelica, 39
Kean, 42
Kelly, Hugh
   A Word to the Wise, 55
Kemble, 101 (48), 110, 111, 124, 134, 136, 137, 141, 154, 155, 157, 160, 163
Kemble, Misses, 113
Kennedy, Mrs., 101
Keyssler, 58
Kielmannsegge, F. Graf von, 28-30, 31, 69 (107)
King, 65, 76, 78, 111, 124, 136
Kleist, Ewald von, 27
Klinger, 1
   Die Zwillinge, 108
Klischnig, 89
Klopstock, 39, 87, 114
Knigge, A. F. F. L., 144 (53)
Knowles, John, 41
Koch, 141
Kotzebue, 73, 123, 128, 141, 153-4, 161
   Das Kind der Liebe, 154, 161
   Menschenhass und Reue, 153, 154, 161
   Rollas Tod, 161 (110)
Küchelbecker, J. B., 13-14, 21
Küttner, K. G., 92-7, 106, 148

la Fite, Mme., 117